PRAISE FOR *THE FIRST SOCIETY*

"Western society is deeply affected, indeed wounded, by sin, by rebellion against God and His plan for our eternal happiness. The most deadly wound has been inflicted by the ferocious attack on the fundamental truth of marriage, which seeks to obscure and sully the sublime beauty of the married state as God intended it from the Creation. Today we must be ready to suffer, as Christians have suffered down the ages, to honor and foster Holy Matrimony. Indeed, as Scott Hahn shows in his inspiring and challenging work, only a society radically obedient, through cooperation with sacramental grace, to the reign of Our Lord, Christ the King, can truly flourish. A society, formed and animated by sacramental grace, is established and flourishes in the very first society, the family. Such a society, in fact, becomes a reality in Christian families who, by their heroic example, witness to the splendor of the truth about marriage."

—RAYMOND LEO CARDINAL BURKE
Member of the Supreme Tribunal of the Apostolic Signatura

"Please don't open *The First Society* expecting a timid sermon. Hahn does not shy away from very direct criticism of secular liberalism as the culprit in undermining both marriage and the just social order. A secular view of marriage, claims Hahn, is as unworkable as a secular view of society. Amen!"

—BENJAMIN WIKER, PHD
Professor of Political Science and Director of Human Life Studies, Franciscan University of Steubenville and author of *In Defense of Nature*

W9-DCE-601

"At a time when legal redefinitions of marriage all over the Western world turn marriage into an utterly private affair, Dr. Hahn convincingly shows how and why marriage is of utmost social and political significance. He does so by demonstrating that the way people live their sexuality has immediate repercussions for the rightly-understood common good. The central thesis of what, according to its author, is not an optimistic, but rather a hope-filled book, is that as Christians, we are allowed to reckon with the power of God who heals our frailty and elevates our nature. Christian marriage, based on the grace of the sacrament, has the power to transform an entire culture as it lays the grounds for authentic solidarity."

—STEPHAN KAMPOWSKI, STD
Professor of philosophical anthropology at the Pontifical John Paul II Institute for Studies on Marriage and Family, Rome, and Co-Author of *Accompanying, Discerning, Integrating*

"In *The First Society*, Scott Hahn delivers the theological insight we've come to expect from him. But he also delivers a practical program for defending the family in our hostile secular world. No more confining ourselves to 'secular' or 'scientific' or 'natural law' reasons for our beliefs. While there is nothing wrong with those reasons, they are not enough. We have been leaving our best player, Jesus, on the bench for far too long. Dr Hahn says "Now is the time to speak Catholic truth with clarity and boldness." I completely agree. Marriage defenders: read this book, and follow its counsels!"

—JENNIFER ROBACK MORSE, PHD
Founder and President of The Ruth Institute

"Scott Hahn does a masterful job of articulating the central role of marriage in God's plan for bringing the world to his heart. *The First Society* is essential reading for anyone who wants to understand why marriage matters—especially in today's world."

—GREGORY POPCAK, PHD
Founder and Executive Director of the Pastoral Solutions Institute and Author of *For Better . . . Forever: The Catholic Guide to Lifelong Marriage*

THE FIRST
SOCIETY

THE FIRST SOCIETY

SOCIETY

The Sacrament of Matrimony and
the Restoration of the Social Order

SCOTT HAHN

EMMAUS
ROAD
PUBLISHING

Steubenville, Ohio
www.EmmausRoad.org

Emmaus Road Publishing
1468 Parkview Circle
Steubenville, Ohio 43952

© 2018 Scott Hahn
All rights reserved. Published 2018.
Printed in the United States of America.

Library of Congress Cataloging-in-Publication Data
Names: Hahn, Scott, author.
Title: The first society : the sacrament of matrimony and the restoration of
the social order / Scott Hahn.
Description: Steubenville : Emmaus Road, 2018.
Identifiers: LCCN 2017054752 (print) | LCCN 2018000888 (ebook) | ISBN
9781947792562 (ebook) | ISBN 9781947792548 (hard cover) | ISBN
9781947792555 (pbk.)
Subjects: LCSH: Marriage--Religious aspects--Christianity. |
Families--Religious aspects--Christianity. | Christianity and culture. |
Catholic Church--Doctrines.
Classification: LCC BV835 (ebook) | LCC BV835 .H344 2018 (print) | DDC
234/.165--dc23
LC record available at https://lccn.loc.gov/2017054752

Unless otherwise noted, Scripture quotations are taken from The Revised
Standard Version Second Catholic Edition (Ignatius Edition). Copyright ©
2006 by the Division of Christian Education of the National Council of the
Churches of Christ in the United States of America. Used by permission. All
rights reserved.

Excerpts from *The Catechism of the Catholic Church*, second edition, copyright © 2000, Libreria Editrice Vaticana—United States Conference of
Catholic Bishops, Washington, D.C. Noted as CCC in the text.

Cover image: *The Marriage of the Virgin* (1644) by Phillipe de Champaigne,
The Wallace Collection, London, UK

Cover design and layout by Margaret Ryland

TABLE OF CONTENTS

To Andrew Jones,
who inspired me to think again about
the shape of a sacramental society.

Introduction

The theme of marriage . . . deserves special attention. The message of the word of God may be summed up in the expression found in the Book of Genesis and taken up by Jesus Himself: "Therefore a man leaves his father and his mother and cleaves to his wife, and they become one flesh" (Gen 2:24; Mk 10:7–8). What does this word say to us today? It seems to me that it invites us to be more aware of a reality, already well known but not fully appreciated: that matrimony is a Gospel in itself, a Good News for the world of today, especially the dechristianized world. The union of a man and a woman, their becoming "one flesh" in charity, in fruitful and indissoluble love, is a sign that speaks of God with a force and an eloquence which in our days has become greater because . . . marriage, in precisely the oldest regions evangelized, is going through a profound crisis. And it is not by chance. Marriage is linked to faith, but not in a general way. Marriage, as a union of faithful and indissoluble love, is based upon the grace that comes from the triune God, who in Christ loved us with a faithful love, even to the Cross. . . . There is a clear link between the crisis in faith and the crisis in marriage. And, as the Church has said and witnessed for a long time now, marriage is called to be not only an object but a subject of the new evangelization.

—Pope Benedict XVI, Homily for the Mass for the Opening of the Synod of Bishops, October 7, 2012

I wasn't even a Catholic yet when I began studying theology at a Catholic university. But it was there, at Marquette University in Milwaukee, that the seed was planted that has come to fruition in this book.

The moment came one day in a graduate seminar, "Religion and Society," taught by a wonderful Jesuit priest, Fr. Donald J. Keefe. Now, I'm sure the class was interesting, but I don't remember the specifics—except for one story. Fr. Keefe was lecturing on *The Naked Public Square* by Rev. Richard John Neuhaus (who was also not yet a Catholic). And then he stopped and stared out the window. As clear as anything I can remember him saying these words: "If Catholics would simply live the Sacrament of Matrimony for one generation, we would witness a transformation of society and have a Christian culture."

Fr. Keefe shook himself out of his musing and returned to his lecture notes, apologizing for his digression. But I could not return my focus so easily. Fr. Keefe might have delivered the rest of the lesson in Swedish as far as I was concerned; I had been transfixed by that offhanded sentence. I could think of nothing else.

All we have to do to achieve the kind of culture we long for is live out the Sacrament of Marriage for a few decades? Could any diagnosis and prescription be simpler and more challenging than this? But it made so much sense. In marriage we find the primordial human community, from which all other communities emerge. If we get marriage right, we can not only transform our families and parishes, we can transform the world.

I was utterly beguiled by this idea, and have been ever since—never more so than when I reflect on my own marriage. At the time of Fr. Keefe's musing, I was exploring the Catholic Church, much to the chagrin of my wife, Kimberly. We had some difficult times ahead as I embraced the Church and she remained skeptical. And yet, despite the challenges, nothing—*nothing*—in my life has brought the deep personal and spiritual fulfillment that marriage and family has.

Yes, I could see then and can see now—better than ever—how marriage could be the key to everything we want to build in our society and culture. But I can also see how daunting, how frightening, and how frustrating—and how unutterably beautiful—the blueprints can be. And so, as I look around at the living fruits of my marriage, I am filled with desire to get to work.

*   *   *

I'm not sure exactly when it happened, but at some point my role in my family shifted, and now I'm *primarily* a grandfather. No father ever stops parenting his children, but I now have fifteen grandchildren scattered around the country; it is these beautiful children who occupy my thoughts when I reflect upon the future.

The timing of this book, then, is primarily inspired by my grandchildren. It's impossible not to consider the future when you hear a newborn's fussy cry. It's impossible not to worry about the society that the next generations will inherit when you are mobbed by toddlers at Christmas. It's impossible not to think about the future of the Church in our culture when you attend their Baptisms and First Communions.

Now, it's popular to frame these concerns in the form of this question: "What kind of society will we leave to our children and grandchildren?" This is a worthy question to consider, to be sure, but I'm not sure it's the *first* question that should occupy us—especially as Catholics trying to navigate an increasingly secular civilization. It's the kind of question that can make you feel helpless and even despairing against the apparent "forces of history."

I remember a conversation with my wife in which she expressed deep concern about the world we are handing down to our children. I responded that, in our role as parents, we are not charged with handing down an entire world or society or culture to our children, but simply the faith. So let us begin by focusing on what is close and dear to us. We can't control the national or civilizational culture our children will inherit, but we *can* do everything in our power to ensure our children will inherit the true faith. We can't control the nature of the society our children will have to contend with, but we *can* influence the nature of the Catholic children our society will have to contend with. In other words, we are transmitting children to our society much more directly than we are transmitting a society to our children.

This is, therefore, a different sort of book for me. As always, you will find in these pages a focus on heaven and eternity, but more than ever I will work through the implications of Catholic teaching in the here and now—what it means to live an authentically Catholic life not just for our souls but for our society. This means I will also have to consider what kind of society most accords with authentic Catholic living.

*   *   *

My grandchildren may have inspired the concept for this book, but the foundations of its arguments have always been present in my other writings and throughout Church teaching. The fact is that I have come to believe strongly that I can no longer leave these implications unsaid. The Sacrament of Matrimony may not be able to transform society in my lifetime, but for those carefree toddlers dancing around the Christmas tree, the beginnings of a more decent, more beautiful, more Catholic culture may still be possible.

Further, when I look beyond my family I see a culture in crisis from top to bottom. This isn't a new development, as we will see later in this book. But the chronic symptoms of a degraded society have, in recent years, become much more acute. In eras of widely shared prosperity and security and good feelings, the social erosion effected by secularism and liberalism can be masked. But in eras of uncertainty and instability, the weakened foundations of our shared life are uncovered—precisely when they are needed most.[1]

Many intelligent Christian writers in recent years have suggested perceptive diagnoses and creative courses of treatment for this malaise. All agree, though, that we have squandered our civilizational patrimony, frittering away the treasury of Christian culture accumulated through the centuries on such ill-conceived vanity projects as the sexual revolution and relativistic mass consumerism. This rejection of the storehouse of Christian values is one of the great tragedies of all of human history since the death and Resurrection of our Lord, and it continues slowly to unfold before our eyes.

While this book, like those works, is certainly a product of and a response to its time and place, I want, however, to stress the timelessness and universality of the ideas on which this book is based. What you'll find in these pages is not so much a diagnosis of *this moment*, but a diagnosis of *what has always been the case* about human societies. It is not so much a prescription for *a new course of action*, but a prescription for *what we could and should have always been*

---

[1] Throughout this book, unless clearly indicated otherwise, the word "liberalism" will refer not to the politics associated with the American Democratic Party or the center-left, broadly speaking, but rather to the dominant theme of Western political thought since the Enlightenment. Liberalism puts the rights and liberties of the individual at the center of the constellation of political values, displacing communal duties and pursuit of the common good. Liberalism therefore conceives of society not as an organic whole with various goods that are proper to that whole, but as a collection of autonomous individuals pursuing their own goods. Secularism is an accelerant for liberalism, eroding the Christian emphasis on truth, love, and service that made liberal societies humane and sustainable.

doing in good times and bad. It is not so much a discovery of *new ways of living*, but a rediscovery of *the resources we have always had* with which to build beautiful and sustainable Christian communities—not just niches tenuously preserved for us by secular benefactors, but entire societies consecrated to Christ.

*   *   *

If this sounds unrealistic, maybe even extravagant, that's because it is. But the unmerited grace of our Lord Jesus Christ mediated through His bride, the Church, is by any human standard unrealistic and extravagant. Ultimately, any "solution" to the problems of this world must begin and end with that grace.

To be clear, then, this is not an *optimistic* book. It does not propose that a new dawn of Christian civilization is just around the corner. It does not suggest that if we squint and look in just the right light, we will see that the twenty-first century is setting up to be a wonderful moment for faithful Catholics in the West. It does not trade in clichéd slogans and easy assurances that wrap naïveté in the twisted garb of false confidence.

This is, rather, a *hope-filled* book. It is about God's grace, the love of Christ, and the life-giving truth of the Church—that which endures and cannot be diminished by social conditions or the supposed "forces of history." It is about that divine patrimony that can never be exhausted and to which, since the advent of the New Covenant, we have always had and will always have access—should we choose to remain in God's friendship. This book, therefore, is fixated on God, the source of hope, because to let our gaze wander is to court despair.

That hope, ultimately, is the hope of heaven—a hope that is realized every time we celebrate the Marriage Supper of the Lamb. The challenge proposed in this book is to bring the superabundance of grace that bubbles forth from the sacramental life of the Church into our families, our communities, our society, and our civilization. The same power that can transform souls can transform the world. It's up to us to bring it to fruition.

CHAPTER 1

No Nostalgia

I had an idyllic childhood. Or at least I've always liked to think so.

When I recently drove a friend through the streets where I was raised, I eagerly pointed out schools, ballfields, and so on, probably boring him with my reminiscing. But he humored me, and soon I was telling him about my old friends as we passed the houses in which they grew up.

As I told my companion what became of my old classmates, the veneer of perfection with which I had covered over my childhood quickly faded. One suffered from alcohol and drug addiction as a young adult. One, we only found out later in life, had been abused. One had taken his own life.

In that moment I was reminded of my own adolescence. I thought about how harrowingly close I had been to ending up someone else's warm memory turned cold—and how fortunate I was to have escaped that fate. And I realized that the problems that haunted those young men didn't just appear out of nowhere. Amid the comfortable trappings of middle-class life, hidden dramas and tragedies had been playing out behind closed doors and within fragile psyches. It just took some time for the decrepit fruits of a deeply corrupt culture to be harvested.

These realizations didn't so much shatter my nostalgia as they complicated it. There was great good in the neighborhood and the relationships of my upbringing, and no amount of new information and rethinking can take that away. And yet no time or place is ever as perfect as we desperately want it to be.

*   *   *

I was born the same month *Leave It to Beaver* debuted on CBS. And I graduated from high school the year *Saturday Night Live* debuted on NBC. Needless to say, my childhood was a time of great cultural change, not unlike what we are going through right now.

To this day, due especially to the popularity of syndicated reruns, *Leave It to Beaver* represents the pinnacle of post–World War II nostalgia. The white picket fence, the safe streets, the basic decency of everyone in the family and in the neighborhood (except Eddie Haskell): it's easy to fall in love with the simple, respectable goodness of that world. How appropriate that Hugh Beaumont, who played Ward Cleaver, was himself a Methodist minister in addition to being an actor!

And yet we know, of course, that this was far from a comprehensive portrait of American life. While Ward played golf at the club in the fictional Mayfield, real black people were being attacked with firehoses by police in Birmingham. While June Cleaver prepared perfect casseroles in perfect Tupperware, the birth control pill was being marketed in the United States for the first time. While Wally and Beaver committed petty shenanigans, the Vietnam War was ramping up and a restless generation was rising. For every perfect family in 1957, there was one broken by abuse, alcoholism, or adultery.

All of these complexities do not void the simple goodness that truly did exist in post–World War II American society, any more than my realizations about my childhood voided the real goodness I experienced. But if we are to learn from the past, we must look at the past as it really was. In our era of rapid social and cultural change and increasing political and economic instability, we cannot afford to be naïve about the lessons we draw from history.

*   *   *

Why all this musing about the past? What's so important about nostalgia? And why should we be concerned about it?

The answer to these questions is the motivation for this book. It's no secret that we are in the midst of a crisis in the public understanding of marriage and family. The headline-grabbing moments in this crisis have been the Supreme Court's decisions in *Windsor v. U.S.* and *Obergefell v. Hodges*, which legally redefined marriage across the country. Now, marriage is *officially* defined as nothing more than a romantic partnership that has been recognized by the state.

But the truth is that these rulings only codified the cultural facts on the ground. The vast majority of Americans already considered marriage nothing more than a government-recognized pact of affection and commitment. Opposition to same-sex marriage evaporated so quickly once the concept gained momentum because the popular understanding of marriage left no principled ground on which to oppose the innovation.

I don't need to remind you of the problems with our marriage culture. One sentence will suffice: divorce is commonplace; young people are delaying marriage or avoiding it altogether; intentionally childless marriages are all the rage; respectable elites are pushing for open and plural marriages; and so on and so forth.

This didn't happen overnight. We have been living for decades as if the hollowed-out version of marriage—the version that says that marriage is a self-defined relationship based on the contingencies of sexual attraction and personal fulfillment with the hope (but not the expectation) of a lifelong commitment—were the real thing. It's in our movies and our television shows, our songs and our books. We can't avoid it any more easily than we can avoid breathing in dust. It's in our social atmosphere.

What this means is that same-sex marriage isn't the cause; it's a symptom. Of course, this particular symptom will, in turn, make the underlying illness worse. *Windsor* and *Obergefell* will acclimate coming generations to this desiccated understanding of marriage not just in practice but in law—and not just in law but in the very Constitution of the United States. (But while we shouldn't overlook the downstream effects of writing modern marriage into the Constitution, we also shouldn't allow ourselves to become preoccupied with them. Same-sex marriage is *part of* a broader problem in our understanding of marriage; it isn't the problem *itself*.)

We are living in a cultural tempest, and so we're looking for a safe harbor. With no apparent deliverance on the horizon, we naturally turn our gaze to the past. Before *Roe v. Wade*. Before no-fault divorce. Before *The Feminine Mystique*. Before the pill. And there, looking back at us with wise and knowing eyes, is Ward Cleaver.

But he is, I'm sorry to say, a mirage.

*　　*　　*

Nostalgia is a humane, even beautiful, emotion. But it can place rose-colored glasses over our eyes—glasses that filter out the difficult and painful realities that might complicate our memory. Therefore, nostalgia cannot be the basis for a sober analysis of our present social and political circumstances, or for a prescription for the future.

I've already pointed out the darker side to the *Leave It to Beaver* era in American history. But a disordered nostalgia doesn't just obscure the past; it can also obscure the present and the future. It's difficult to have a clear vision of where we are or where we're going if we idealize where we've been.

The idealized object of our nostalgia can become a false starting point—a false blank slate onto which we project current problems. If, for instance, we identify 1957 as the ideal moment in American society, then we have ruled out trends that predate 1957, not to mention countercurrents and undercurrents in 1957 life, from our analysis.

That's not how human society works. Every era has its good and bad points, and every era builds on or responds to its predecessors. During the French Revolution, the revolutionaries tried to create a new calendar with the first year of the new republic designated Year 1. The conceit was that the French Republic represented such a break with the past that a new and totally distinct era of human history had begun. But history was not so accommodating: the calendar lasted only a little longer than the First Republic itself—about a dozen years.

The 1950s cannot be isolated from their context. All the qualities we associate with that era were contingent on long-term trends in politics, economics, and culture, such as post–World War II prosperity and social retrenchment. But at the same time, despite the staid world of Mayfield portrayed in *Leave It to Beaver*, sexual mores were loosening. Hugh Hefner, for instance, founded *Playboy* in 1953.

This search for historical perfection doesn't stop in the 1950s, though. Some Catholics point instead to the Middle Ages as a period with a social order we should try to recapture. (I'll discuss this era later, but suffice it to say now that it was a more complicated time than either sneering modernists or doe-eyed traditionalists want to believe.) Others think that if we could just un-ring the bell of the Progressive movement at the turn of the twentieth century, we could be enjoying a beautiful, liberal, Christian civilization today.

These idealizations of the past don't exactly qualify as nostalgia because no one today was actually around to experience those historical moments. But the impulse is the same—to identify a historical social order to which we should return in order to create a sustainable and virtuous society.

This isn't sober analysis, but escapism. The search for a perfect moment in history is like the search for the Loch Ness Monster: it isn't there, and if you try to fake it, everyone will see right through it. That's the thing about nostalgia: no two persons' stories and memories are the same, and so no two experiences of nostalgia are the same. Nostalgia is a deeply personal emotion, so it cannot be the basis for political discourse, let alone a political order.

For every person who can relate to your feelings about, say, the early 1960s, there are several for whom your account will lack all credibility. This could be due to differences in race, class, or sex. Or it could just be diverse minds remembering in distinct ways.

But even if we could find some perfect moment in history, the sad truth—the real sting of nostalgia—is that we could not return.

*   *   *

The word "nostalgia" comes from Greek words that combine to mean the pain associated with a desire to return home. Whether our cultural nostalgia is for a time we personally experienced or for a time before we were born, it is ultimately a longing to "return" to a time and place where our values and way of life would be welcomed and nourished. That is, it's a desire to return home.

There is hardly anything more human than the desire to be home. It ties in with so many of our natural desires. We want to be attached to a place that existed before us and will exist after us. We want our stories to be woven into larger stories—of families, places, events, and so on—

through time. We want to love and to be loved by those closest to us.

What we must realize, however, is that all of these desires are but reflections of the ultimate desire of every human person: eternal communion with God in heaven—our true home. Only in heaven will all our longings be fulfilled. Only in heaven will we feel finally, truly, totally at home.

This is the tragedy of all nostalgia, especially nostalgia for a *time* and not just a place: it can never actually be satisfied in this life. We can experience bits and pieces of nostalgic fulfillment—a classic TV show here, a memorable aroma there—but on this earth we can never experience complete, sustainable fulfillment.

This doesn't make nostalgia bad. It does mean, though, that we must put it in its proper place. Nostalgia, like all passions, must remain subservient to reason in our psyches. And it certainly cannot be the basis for cultural, social, and political renewal. That is a burden nostalgia simply cannot bear.

Furthermore, the peculiarities of our moment in history also make attempts to recreate the past—even the recent past—a quixotic venture.

*   *   *

More than at any time in Western history, we live in a secularized society. Even late Roman society, while decadent and in many ways grotesque, valued public piety (even if it was pagan piety, and even if it was just as an expression of allegiance to the empire). But now Western civilization not only shuns all religious expression from the public square, but has also intentionally set about dismantling its own Christian heritage.

The Christian patrimony is, on the one hand, inexhaustible. The Truth can never run out. We can't use up Christ's love or God's grace. These supernatural goods are infinite and eternal. As we consider what the next move should be for Christians in this civilization, we must never forget this.

On the other hand, though, we can use up our Christian *cultural* patrimony. Indeed, the well is nearly dry. Precious few people have any concept of what a truly and comprehensively Christian society would look like. And this isn't just about things we're used to calling "culture"—art and music and architecture and so on. It's also about Christian political and social understandings, such as the primacy of the common good, the essential role of the Church in public life, and the inalienable dignity of the person. While these truths, like everything else in the treasury of Church teaching, never change, they can be lost, or at least forgotten, for a time.

Any discussion of what Christians should be aiming for in re-forming society must take account of where we are now. The Middle Ages, the nineteenth century, and even the 1950s relied on substantial reserves of Christian culture that we simply do not have any longer. *Even if* any previous era could be considered comprehensively good enough to emulate, we don't have the resources of our Christian patrimony with which to do it. Laying the foundation not just to recover that patrimony but to earn a new patrimony for the twenty-first century and beyond must be at the heart of this discussion.

Secularism has placed the past more out of reach than

ever. This moment, therefore, presents us with new challenges that will require new and innovative responses. But just because we can't recreate the past doesn't mean we can't learn from it.

*   *   *

A healthy relationship with the past will neither worship it nor ignore it. Rather, as we look back to times and places we both admire and disdain, our rule should be simple: take the best; leave the rest.

There was real good in the 1950s, in the Middle Ages, and in whatever other era we might admire. Our prudential task is not only to disentangle the good from the bad, but to discern what can be effectively applied to our current historical moment—and how to do it.

We can find reflections of timeless truths in every historical era. Each era applies its own filters to create those reflections, so it's up to us to discern what the complete image looks like, and then how it might apply to a post-modern world.

For instance, we can see a strong reflection of Christian anthropology in the focus on the nuclear family and gender norms in 1950s America. But it's important to remember that these were *only* reflections; these concepts can quickly become idols that obscure more than reveal the truth.

Let's look at the nuclear family. Its dominance is a relatively modern and unbiblical phenomenon that represents something quite good—the importance of stable relationships between parents and their children to the sustainability of society itself. But it can also obscure the importance of the extended, transgenerational family that had been the historical norm, and, instead, favor a limited understanding of family identity and duties. The question then is: How do we apply the truth represented by 1950s' family life to the twenty-first century without falling into crude idolization and sentimentalism?

Similarly, the preeminence of the Church in every area of life through most of the Middle Ages is a clear reflection of the truth that the sacramental logic of the Church can and should be applied throughout society. And yet anyone with a passing knowledge of medieval history knows that this preeminence often bred great corruption in the Church. Given that we do not want to recreate a necessarily idealized past time, we have several questions to guide us: How can we apply the sacramental logic of the faith to the peculiar circumstances of the twenty-first century while learning from the pitfalls of the past? How can the Church use this logic not just to speak to secularism but to defeat it? Can we find here the intellectual and spiritual resources for a rebirth of Christian civilization?

Much of the rest of this book will consider the answers to these questions. Let's begin, however, by going back to the very beginning, to the first marriage of the first human beings.

CHAPTER 2

The First Society

It is one of the most important pivot points in the Bible: "It is not good that the man should be alone" (Gen 2:18). Until this point in the twofold creation account—the six days of Genesis 1 and the garden of Genesis 2 and 3—God had announced that every aspect of His creation was "good," or in the case of mankind, "very good." But here, for the very first time, the Lord says that something in His creation is "not good": loneliness.

Everything had seemed to be complete and in place. Adam had a home in the garden, all the food and water he could eat and drink, and more pets than he knew what to do with. More than that, he had God, in whose image and likeness he had been made. And yet neither creation nor Adam himself were complete. He was alone, and it was not good.

We all know what happens next: God tranquilizes Adam and removes a rib. He uses that bone as the first piece of the only being suitable as a companion for the man—a woman. As Adam says, "This at last is bone of my bones and flesh of my flesh" (Gen 2:23). Humanity was now complete. The full image and likeness of God had been fulfilled.

But there's more. Eve wasn't just the first woman; she completed the *first family*. The first human community created by God was not a pair of roommates or simple friends, but a married couple. The union of man and woman as husband and wife (and, God willing, father and mother) is the very foundation of not just every human society, but of all humanity.

God's order of creation was not arbitrary. We were created for community; that is, our nature finds its fullest expression in community with other persons. Aristotle got it right even without divine revelation: man is a social being. As it was at the beginning, so it remains today: the family is the *first society*, both in order of time and of importance.

*   *   *

The idea of the atom—an indivisible, discrete unit of matter—was postulated as far back as the ancient world. Scientists only discovered real evidence for the theory in the early nineteenth century, and for the better part of one hundred years they supposed atoms were the smallest particles in the universe.

We now know about electrons and protons and neutrons and Higgs bosons and any number of other subatomic particles. But in an important respect, the theory of the ancients and the model of the early scientists holds true: atoms are the smallest unit of matter that retain all the properties of an element. And so while atoms may not be the smallest particles in the universe, they are the fundamental units of matter.

Scientists were accumulating evidence for atomic theory as other thinkers were formulating new ways to consider human societies. These new liberal ideas emphasized the individual rather than the family, clan, or community. Today we take for granted the preeminence of the individual; that is, we take for granted that the fundamental unit of society is the individual. Sociologists borrow a term from science to describe the breaking apart of civil society brought on by this individualism: *atom*ization.

While we mustn't ignore the importance of the individual, the truth is that reducing society to a collection of unattached individuals would be like trying to reduce nature to a collection of unattached atoms. It doesn't get us very far. Sure, we'd have gold and nitrogen and even diamonds (which are just well-organized carbon). But we wouldn't have water or sugars or proteins, all of which are essential to life, and all of which are molecules—combinations of atoms. Even oxygen gas is a mash-up of two oxygen atoms, not individual particles floating in space.

Likewise, nobody goes through life all alone. We have communities of personal friends and school peers and work colleagues. We bond over sports teams and TV shows. We depend on each other for help in hard times, both personally or through systems of social support. And, of course, we worship together—though not as much as we used to.

But, most fundamentally, we are born into a community—the community of (ideally) mother, father, and child. No one—not even Jesus Christ—has ever been spawned fully-formed as a radical individual. We are born, totally helpless, into community. That community is what we call a family. And while the fundamental unit of humanity might be the individual, the fundamental unit of society is the family.

*   *   *

Every family, every community, and every society begins, in some way or another, with a man and a woman—an Adam and an Eve. This is how God created us. It is, in fact, how we share most fully His image and likeness, as Genesis tells us: "So God created man in his own image, in the image of God he created him; male and female he created them" (Gen 1:27).

Earlier I said that the married couple is the first society in order of time and importance. But what, exactly, does that mean?

Let's start with the order of time. Most obviously this means that, at the very beginning in the garden, God gave the man not a colleague or a mentor but a wife. God could have established any kind of relationship first among His new creations, but He decided on marriage. This was not arbitrary. He was signaling that, for His prized creation, the union of man and woman was of particular and enduring value.

But the concept of the married couple as a place of beginnings didn't end in the garden. With every marriage, something brand new is established. God may not be rearranging body parts, as He did when He made Eve, but He is, in a real way, rearranging our souls. Every married couple is a new creation: "Therefore a man leaves his father and his mother and clings to his wife, and they become one flesh" (Gen 2:24).

The consummation of the marriage is, in a real and radical way, a new beginning—the creation of a new family that is a reflection of the original creation of all humanity, except this time we participate *with* God. Whether or not God blesses the union with children, the couple has created something new that has never been before or will be again. This participation in God's creative power is the foundation of human society.

For this reason, the married couple is first not just in time but in importance. Without the uniquely creative power God has bestowed on that relationship, there can be no further community, no self-sustaining society. Therefore we must treat marriage with particular care and concern; we can say without disparaging other types of relationships that nothing has so much riding on it as marriage does. There is no substitute for the union of a man and woman as husband and wife.

A society where strong and loving friendships fail to form is weakened. A society where trusting work partnerships fail to form is impoverished. A society where marriages fail to form, on the other hand, is on the road to extinction.

*   *   *

DNA is essentially the blueprint for all the incredibly complicated molecules that living cells have to make. If cells fail to produce certain organic molecules, or if the molecules they produce are misshapen or wrongly formulated, then any number of disorders—and even death—can result.

This, by the way, is how radiation poisoning works. Tiny particles pass through the body, but smack into strands of

DNA on the way, knocking things out of place. Radiation smudges the blueprints, which results in mutations—unpredictable and unfixable changes that are passed down in the creation of new DNA. When too many blueprints are smudged, the errors accumulate until the body simply cannot function any longer.

If culture is the DNA of a society—where the blueprints come from—it is in marriage where the instructions are executed. Unlike individual cells, though, married couples can tinker with the blueprints. They can discern whether changes are helpful or dangerous, and react accordingly. They can, uniquely, both form and execute the DNA of society.

Marriage is where most of the essential human elements of society are built. I don't just mean individual children. As I said, marriage permits us to participate in the creative power of God in the formation and maintenance of new communities as well as new individuals. When marriage is not performing this function or is performing it poorly, the entire social body suffers.

When marriages are weak or fail to form at all, parents (especially isolated mothers) are helpless against the prevailing cultural DNA. Without the social and sacramental strength of marriage, it's incredibly difficult to do anything other than execute the instructions provided by the culture. Families become subject to the ebb and flow of trends and fads. More often than not, harmful mutations in the DNA just compound one another generation after generation.

And what about when marriages form but the individuals who make up the marriage are themselves malformed? While this situation is more stable than a society with a weak or nonexistent marriage culture, it is hardly less dangerous.

Malformed marriages will make imprudent adjustments to the cultural DNA. They will accept what should be rejected and reject what should be accepted. Harmful mutations will go uncorrected.

The problem is that our society is bathed in dangerous radiation. It is everywhere around us. It is in us. And it is jumbling up our social DNA in ways so complex (and often hidden) that we can't fully grasp it. And yet we, somehow, have to react.

Catholics have an advantage, though. In the timeless teaching of Christ and the Church, we have DNA that is impervious even to the strongest and most dangerous cultural radiation. Let's consider two aspects of the Church's DNA for marriage, family, and society: the Trinitarian and sacramental nature of marriage.

*   *   *

It was "not good" for Adam to be alone. But why? Was it just the emotional state of loneliness that God found troubling? Or was there something deeper—something in the nature of man and God itself?

We worship, in the words of the Athanasian Creed, "one God in Trinity, and Trinity in Unity, neither confounding the Persons, nor dividing the Essence." This Trinitarian mystery—how can God be *both* one *and* three?—is at the heart of our faith.

Whatever else we might say about this incredible mystery, this much is clear: God is both unity and community. Within God are both the concept of oneness and the concept of togetherness. Further, these concepts are not in contradiction or even competition; rather, they complement and complete each other.

This is why Adam's loneliness was "not good." He wasn't just emotionally incomplete; he was incomplete in his very creation as a being in God's likeness. To be truly made in God's image means to be an individual in community.

And marriage, as I've said, is the first human community. It is the fundamental way we participate in God's Trinitarian essence. This doesn't mean that celibate priests and religious and single persons don't participate in earthly reflections of the Trinity; everyone is a member of some community or another, whether secular or religious, that brings our natural orientation to togetherness to life.

Marriage does this, however, in a unique and special way: "they become one flesh." Nowhere else in the Scriptures is a phrase of such radical unity-in-community used in reference to human beings. The capacity of marriage to bring forth children completes the Trinitarian analogy: mother, father, children.

And what is it that sustains the family? The mutual love of all members for one another. When all else fails—when finances run short, when teenage hormones run wild, when tempers run hot—this mutual love keeps that unity-in-community together.

And this mutual love, perhaps more than anything else, reflects the essence of God. We say with conviction and truth that "God is love." But love requires both a subject and an object—a giver and a receiver. Of course, God's love is poured out for us, the pinnacle of His creation. But while that fact would justify the statement "God loves," it doesn't fully explain the deeper claim that God *is* love.

We can say that God *is* love because He is, in His very self, both the subject and the object of love. The Father, the Son, and the Holy Spirit—each of whom are fully God Himself—are in an eternal relationship of love with one another. This perpetual self-giving is what makes God who He is. And it is what marriage reflects, imperfectly but beautifully, in this world.

*   *   *

Many generations before the founding of the Catholic Church by Jesus Christ, God the Father indicated the sacramental nature of marriage in His relationship with Adam and Eve. The coming together of man and woman as husband and wife has been, from the very beginning, blessed by God in a special way.

The English word "sacrament" comes from the Latin *sacramentum*, which means "bond" or "oath." Throughout Scripture, the oath—sworn on the name of God Himself—appears time and again as an essential element of covenants. In fact, later in the Old Testament when an angel of God announces the covenant with Abraham, he declares that the Lord is making an oath on His own name (Gen 22:16–18).

And what do we mean by "covenant"? It is helpful to contrast the concept with "contract," with which it is easily confused. A contract generally sets the terms of giving, taking, or sharing certain aspects of ourselves—property, goods, labor, and so on. A covenant, on the other hand, sets the terms of joining our *entire selves* with another. A covenant builds on a contract to such a degree that it becomes something truly and substantially different.

"Covenant," then, is the only word that will do to describe the relationship between God and humanity. We are not His property; we are His adopted sons and daughters. Contracts create temporary and contingent arrangements of property; covenants create permanent family bonds.

Adam and Eve's relationship with each other and with the Lord had all the hallmarks of a covenant sealed by an oath—a *sacramentum*. The first two humans were not just lovers: they were sacramentally bound together. That is to say, they were married. And from that covenant all of humanity came forth.[1]

And here's the really beautiful part of this particular sacramental bond: according to the ancient rabbis, it was sealed on the very day that is the sign of God's covenant with all humanity—the Sabbath. In the first chapter of Genesis, God puts all the pieces of the universe together in the first six days, but creation isn't complete until His day of rest. Of course, God never *needs* to rest. But this seventh day—this Sabbath—is an invitation for humanity to take a rest ourselves and therefore to participate in the inner life of God.

Adam and Eve's marriage is sealed on the day that is the very sign of God's covenant with the pinnacle of His creation. This sacramental bond lays the foundation not just for all future generations of humanity, but for all future covenants—both among people and between God and His people. Marriage isn't just the first human society; it is, in a sense, the first sacrament.

---

[1] See John Grabowski, *Sex and Virtue: An Introduction to Sexual Ethics* (Washington, DC: Catholic University of America Press, 2002).

*   *   *

Marriage, then, is the first and fundamental society. From marriage all other societies spring forth and take their structure. This intrinsic connection between marriage and society suggests that the Trinitarian and sacramental natures of marriage have something to teach us about human societies generally.

The Trinitarian aspect of marriage teaches us that we most fully participate in God's likeness when we are in community with others. Remember that aloneness was the first part of creation the Lord announced to be "not good." The community is not, to the Catholic understanding, an unnecessary limitation on our personality and individuality. Rather, a proper society helps us to actualize our true selves: beings made to seek the Lord, to find Him, and to spend eternity united to Him.

Similarly, the sacramental nature of marriage points to the divine orientation of human society. Marriage is a covenantal relationship that reflects God's covenant with mankind (and with the Church, in particular). In the same way, society ought to recognize and reflect our covenantal duties to the Lord. It would be quite strange if communities based in the sacramental institution of marriage were just secular inventions with no orientation toward God and the good. It would be more than strange; it wouldn't make any sense at all.

This is what the rest of this book will be about: the implications of the truth of marriage for society and the state. But first let's examine the cultural history of marriage, where we see this truth consistently recognized but always imperfectly applied.

CHAPTER 3

A Marriage-Haunted Society

I grew up in Pittsburgh, not far from the town of Ambridge, Pennsylvania, which is said to have once had both more churches and more bars per capita than any town in America.

Incorporated in 1905 as a company town of the American Bridge Company (hence the name), Ambridge sits a little more than fifty miles up the Ohio River from my current home in Steubenville, Ohio. Like most of the towns of these river valleys, Ambridge has been leaking population and industry for decades. About one-third as many people live in Ambridge as did in 1930.

Without people to fill them, many of the churches and, yes, even some of the bars are now closed and empty. The shells of the churches are obvious enough; the bars require a bit more observation—a broken sign here, a fractured glass block window there.

And yet—and this is my point—the infrastructure of Ambridge gives us an idea of what previous generations of residents valued: worship and conviviality. At the end of long days in the mills and factories, they would gather around the cup of the Lord and glasses of Iron City—the local swill. Even in disrepair, the institutions built by the people of this town endure in recognizable ways.

I could go on and on. Nearly every corner, for instance, seems to have an open or long-closed lodge of a fraternal association: elk or moose or lions or some other large mammal. These institutions remind us of the importance of mutual social and financial support to people whose livelihoods were often totally dependent on the business cycle.

It would be too much to say that Ambridge is a ghost town, but it is haunted, in a sense, by the economic and social conditions of its past. The town was built for a different time, and we can learn about that time by observing what has endured—especially what no longer seems to make sense in our postmodern world.

Our society is haunted by the culture of marriage and family that used to give it form and structure. So much of what we are accustomed to about living in modern America only makes sense in the context of such a culture. And yet that culture is gone and the infrastructure, human and architectural, remains. In this chapter we'll look at what happens when marriage decays like the factories of the Ohio River Valley.

*　　*　　*

In the previous chapter, I described marriage as the "first society," because it is the basic human community from which all others spring forth. We can also think of this concept of the "first society" in another way: the family is the first society children are aware of and a part of. This first community in which children are raised will prepare them, well or poorly, for participation in all the larger communities they will inhabit for the rest of their lives.

This is what we mean when we say that families give a society its form and structure. The buildings you can construct with Tinker Toys are different from those you can construct with Legos. And regardless of the brand name of the toy, crooked and misshapen pieces will result in unstable structures. The raw materials determine to a great extent what the final product will look like. The family, then, shapes and churns out the raw materials of society. How well (or poorly) families do this job will determine the structure and the stability of the wider community.

While man is naturally a social creature ("It is not good for the man to be alone"), this aspect of our nature is in constant tension with the self-centeredness that is the fruit of the Fall and of our everyday sinfulness. One of the most important roles the family plays is as the first place where young people grow accustomed to considering the needs of other individuals and the community ahead of themselves.

This formation of young people begins with the relationship between husband and wife. Mom and Dad are the first people every child gets to know; parents provide children with the first experience of what living in community requires. If parents demonstrate the priority of each other's needs and their shared goals over their own concerns, that family spirit will shape the way their children conceive of social responsibilities later on. Conversely, if parents act like individuals pursuing their own ends who just happen to live under the same roof, that individualism will filter down.

The ethic of mutual responsibility that is formed in families is the connective tissue of society. When this connective tissue is weak, no matter how strong and independent individual members are, the movement of the whole body toward common ends will be awkward, halting, or even impossible. (I'll discuss the importance of the common good in Catholic social thought later in this book.) This is what happens when marriages fail to form or are infected with the spirit of radical individualism.

On the other hand, when this connective tissue is strong—when young people are formed with a strong ethic of shared responsibility for the good of all members of the community and the community as a whole—the social body moves toward common goals with ease and grace. Even when some individual members are weak and dependent, they are confidently supported by those around them. This is what happens when marriages are plentiful and strong.

All human societies eventually take on the form and structure of the families that comprise them. A disintegrating culture of marriage will lead to a disintegrating society. But you don't have to take my word for it. Just look around.

*   *   *

I opened this book by declaring that this is no time for nostalgia. Even so, we can look around us and see the echoes of a culture that valued and lived out marriage far better than we do now. While we can't go back, we can learn from these observations about how a society takes on the shape of its families.

Go to just about any neighborhood built more than a

couple generations ago and you'll see a place built not for atomized individuals, but for *families* who lived interconnected lives. Whether in the city or the suburbs, you'll find houses and streets and sidewalks and public spaces suitable for walking to visit friends, to go to the lunch counter, or to play in open space. This wasn't because adults desired "walkable communities" as a personal lifestyle choice; it was, at least in part, because it only made sense when the streets were teeming with children to build spaces suited to their limited modes of transportation! (Modern walkable developments, though built to mimic the neighborhoods of the past, still end up looking different because they are built to accommodate a less marriage-oriented society. For instance, the public spaces in these new neighborhoods are more likely to be paved plazas suitable for sipping coffee, rather than open spaces suitable for children's games of cops and robbers.)

Perhaps the most obvious example of the ruins of a marriage-oriented culture is in the Church itself. In any American city that reached maturity earlier than the last few decades, you'll see the shells of Catholic churches. And it's often not just churches in disuse: you can see schools, convents, and rectories, all no longer needed. Sometimes they're vacant; sometimes they're reused respectfully; sometimes, tragically, they're reused blasphemously.

Some of this change, of course, is simply due to shifts in population distributions. But that doesn't explain the raw decrease in the numbers of Catholics across entire regions, and it certainly doesn't explain the collapse in vocations to the priesthood and religious life across the board.

The truth is that Catholics have participated in the

breakdown of our marriage culture just as surely as any other group. Our own infrastructure was built for a culture that produced enough children from intact families to fill up beautiful large churches and schools and convents and rectories. These children learned about the faith and developed a distinctive Catholic identity through family and community traditions and dedication to the faith.

This process of identity formation, it turns out, is one of the more serious casualties of the loss of a marriage culture.

*   *   *

You can never quote just one word of a piece of literature. Well, you could, but no one would know what you were talking about. While every word has its own individual definition, words are given a great deal of their meaning by the other words around them. A *bucket* full of soapy water submerging a mop and a *bucket* full of cement encasing a snitch's feet conjure very different images and emotions in a reader or listener.

Put succinctly: words require context. Every word is part of a phrase; every phrase is part of a sentence; every sentence is part of a paragraph; every paragraph is part of a larger story. Each level of this chain of language takes on meaning from the context provided by higher levels. The result isn't just a narrative or an argument, but a kind of ecosystem. Every part depends for its meaning, in at least some way, on every other part.

This is similar to how humans form our identities. We all have aspects of our identity that are truly our own, but the majority of our identity comes from our context—the individuals we spend time with and the communities we are a part of.

Just think about all the words you'd use to describe yourself, from sports fandom to political and religious beliefs. With the exception of basic personality and character traits, everything that contributes to our identity comes from communities with which we are affiliated in some way—our family, our neighborhood, our city, our political party, our ethnic or national background, and, most importantly, our Church. What those aspects of our identity mean to us, then, is affected by these communities and the people who make them up.

We are part of a social ecosystem; it's only natural that we form our sense of self—our identity—from the persons, communities, and institutions in that ecosystem that give our lives structure and meaning. And marriage is the lynchpin of this ecosystem.

This is exactly what the sociologist Robert Nisbet taught in his landmark book *The Quest for Community*. Nisbet recognized that communities that serve important social functions in our lives, such as families and parishes and social clubs, give structure to our day-to-day living, and thus contribute to our identity. But when the functions of these communities fade or are replaced, such as by the government, their strength as identity-forming institutions fades as well.

Nisbet recognized all the way back in 1953 that the trend in modern Western societies was toward the disintegration of the communities that give us structure and identity—beginning with marriage. More than sixty years later, we're experiencing the latest and perhaps terminal phase of this process of disintegration. As our traditional identity-forming institutions have withered, where have we looked to form our identities? In our deeply individualistic culture, the first place to look was easy: inside ourselves.

*　　*　　*

Since God created Eve, no human being has ever lived truly alone—and even before Eve, Adam had God right there at hand. Aristotle taught centuries before Christ and more than a millennium before St. Thomas Aquinas that man is a social animal—that we are meant to live *together* and to work for *each other's* good. Even in this age of disintegration and individualism, everyone starts life with at least one other person: a mother.

And yet the craze of the moment is "self-identification," and three words that would've been incomprehensible even a few decades ago now easily roll off the tongue: "I identify as . . ." The idea is that we can all decide for ourselves what will constitute our identity: which sexual attractions, which gender, and even, in especially weird cases, which race. We believe we can create meaning for ourselves all by ourselves, without reference to any other person, community, or institution. We think we can be all alone and, strangely, we think it's good to be all alone.

But in truth, identity is almost always a *participation in* and *addition to* a story bigger than ourselves. "Hahn" is a German name, and so in at least some attenuated fashion I *participate in* and *add to* the German American experience; what I can't do is decide all by myself what it means to be a German American or that I don't want to be a German American any longer. That would require a narcissism that would make Narcissus himself blush.

The same is true of smaller everyday communities. Everybody's family, no matter how dysfunctional, forms them in some way that can neither be chosen nor completely undone. We are all the product of communities—even if just the community of a mother and her child.

The truth is that radical self-identification is impossible. It's simply not how human beings were created. Rather than being liberated, the uprooted individual finds himself naked against the overwhelming power of much larger, less organic, and often less well-intentioned identity-forming institutions.

*   *   *

Robert Nisbet wrote his most enduring work in the aftermath of the rise and fall of European fascism, and during the long tyranny of Soviet communism. And so when he looked for institutions that sought to replace disintegrated marriages and marriage-oriented communities, he naturally looked to the state. That is, he saw in mid-twentieth-century totalitarianism the fruits of the breakdown of civil society.

We all desire to participate in a story—an identity— bigger than ourselves. This is part of what it means to be a social creature. But it's also a reflection of our natural desire to participate in God's life. It's built into our nature.

Individualism leaves us cold. Individually and as a society, we get a temporary high from a feeling of liberation, but then the realization sets in: What now? Where do we find meaning? Of what stories are we a part? In what context do we place our individuality?

Nisbet points to the state. Once all the intermediate institutions of civil society have been gutted, we find meaning, purpose, and identity in the state—in its authority, in its stability, and in the grand myths (often exclusionary ethnic myths) it constructs about itself. The state becomes the primary source of identity for an uprooted people.

We can and should expand this analysis, though. In an era of global, hegemonic consumer capitalism, the institutions of the market provide another source of identity formation. At one point these institutions were largely local in nature—mom-and-pop stores and so on—and so they made up part of the patchwork of civil society that formed identities and *insulated* individuals from power. Now, by creating and enforcing brand loyalty to multinational corporations and making livelihoods completely dependent on such organizations, the market has become just as distant, impersonal, and imperious as the state.

More than that, modern entanglements between powerful business interests and the administrative state mean that the civil authorities and profit-seeking corporations are often in cahoots: they have a *shared* interest in making individuals dependent on the state *and* the market (or at least preferred interests within the marketplace) for identity and even existence. When marriage—the connective tissue of civil society—disintegrates, the state and the market are the only games left in town.

This may bring an initial feeling of stability, even permanency. After all, compared to local parishes and social clubs and even spouses, the federal bureaucracy and McDonald's and Proctor & Gamble feel eternal and unchanging—almost like God Himself. But it turns out this arrangement isn't sustainable at all.

*   *   *

We live in a time marked by unease and insecurity. It's not just the fear of war or terrorism; it's the fear of losing a job or having an expensive health crisis. It's the experience of treading water and never knowing when the next wave is coming.

There's nothing new about political and economic insecurity, and in truth things have been a lot worse than they are now. But the sensation of unease is undoubtedly more acute and more widespread than it has been at any time in at least a generation.

One of the main reasons for this subjective unease and the objective political and economic instability that has accompanied it is the collapse of a culture of marriage. As I've said many times (it is, after all, a main theme of this book), God made us to be interdependent. The mutual dependency of human beings, expressed most fully in marriage, is both a dim reflection of the relationship among the persons of the Trinity and a reminder of our ultimate dependence on that Trinity. We can't go it alone (and shouldn't try to) because we weren't made to go it alone.

When the spirit of marriage and family is replaced by the spirit of individualism, our dependency doesn't vanish; rather, it's transferred. We become dependent on fewer people and institutions that are more distant and less caring than the messy patchwork of organic civil society. These distant institutions—governments and corporations and so on—are perceived to be stable, but that stability is bureaucratic and impersonal. They will continue to exist, even prosper, whether you do or not. Our well-being—physical, financial, emotional—increasingly feels like it's subject to the whims of forces we cannot control. *Mutual* dependency has been replaced by the *one-way* dependence of the less powerful on the more powerful.

In the Christian vision of society, we are to be Jesus to one another. That's mutuality. In the individualistic society, distant and powerful institutions don't act like God, but instead try to *replace* Him. That's servitude. Unlike the loving God who created and adopted us into His very family, the god of governments and markets is self-serving and uncaring. It's not how human beings were meant to live, and so we shouldn't be surprised if it feels, in ways difficult to describe but impossible to ignore, unnatural, alien, and frightening. And that's why it can't last.

CHAPTER 4

Marriage Is Impossible

Joseph Heller published *Catch-22* in 1961—during the rapid cultural change that marked my childhood. Heller courted controversy and anticipated the coming anti-war movement by using World War II—the archetype of the virtuous American military intervention—as the backdrop for his story of the absurdity of war in the bureaucratic era.

It was a book well-suited to the emerging uncertainty about and questioning of traditional norms and structures of power. Although it is held in suspicion by many for that reason, Heller's "catch-22" concept can teach us something important about the absurdity of the secular liberal culture from which it emerged.

The term "catch-22" has entered the American vocabulary to describe an unsolvable problem—specifically a problem where the only solution is prohibited by something in the rules of the problem itself. In the novel, Heller describes the bureaucratic guidelines governing flying missions into Europe from a Mediterranean base: if you're mentally unstable, you don't have to fly missions; but if you request an exemption from flying, that demonstrates that you are, in fact, mentally stable enough to fly. So there's no way out.

Secularism poses just such a catch-22 for society. We have a problem, namely a society that has been gutted of its very substance: stable marriages and enduring family ties. The solution, of course, is a reemergence of a robust culture of marriage, where husbands and wives are supported in their vocation to a permanent covenant of faithfulness and, God willing, childbearing. Nothing short of this will do.

But this will require more than having nice marriages portrayed on sitcoms and government programs to counsel young couples. It will also require a public understanding of the *sacramentality* of marriage—that marriage is more than just a notarized contract, but a covenant in which the Lord of Heaven and Earth participates. But secularism, which insists on a public square totally voided of religious ideas and commitments, cannot abide this. Secularism not only corrodes the connective tissue of society; it also makes it impossible to replace.

*　　*　　*

In the movie *The Princess Bride*, the self-absorbed antagonist Vizzini has a habit of exclaiming "Inconceivable!" at moments when that word isn't quite appropriate. Inigo Montoya, one of the heroes of the fairy tale, eventually gets fed up and calmly informs him, "You keep using that word. I do not think it means what you think it means."

It's one of the most famous lines of the film, and maybe one of the most-quoted movie lines of the last generation—

not least because it can be applied in so many circumstances. We can all think of times when we didn't fully understand a word or concept we used, and how the confusion that resulted was sometimes funny (like the contrast between the over-the-top Vizzini and the deadpan Inigo Montoya), but sometimes disruptive and even dangerous.

We conceive of reality through words; if we use words imprecisely or improperly, it can change the way we view ourselves and the world around us. This can also work the other way: the way we live influences how we think about the words and concepts that describe our experience.

Such is the case with marriage. We talk about it all the time because, even for the unmarried, it's so much a part of our lives. But do we fully understand what we're describing when we say the word "marriage"? Like Inigo Montoya, I'm here to tell you: you keep using that word. It does not mean what you think it means.

It's not your fault—well, at least not totally. The truth is that the way our culture has practiced marriage has been so far from the full reality of the institution—especially the *sacramental* nature of the institution—for so long that the prevailing understanding of marriage has become nearly unrecognizable. It's gotten so bad that most people think marriage has no nature at all—they think that it's just whatever we make of it. The only boundaries are bureaucratic logistics and our imagination. Marriage is everything, and therefore it is nothing.

But even when we have a firm idea of what marriage is, it's usually as a civil institution first, with a "religious" element layered on top. The "real" marriage is logged in the county courthouse somewhere, and the sacrament is a nice bonus. This is in part why the recent crisis of the political understanding of marriage has been so challenging: since our conception of marriage was tied primarily to the civil law, changes in that law have impacted the view of the institution itself.

But let's stipulate that marriage has a nature outside of the civil law—that is, that the state has a duty to recognize and protect the truth of marriage rather than define it willy-nilly. Where does that nature come from? Is it implied in the facts of human nature—our biology and orientation toward community and our pursuit of goods we can discern with our reason? Or is the nature of marriage truly supernatural—defined and ordained by God in His revelation of truth to mankind?

* * *

Marriage is, first of all, a natural institution. It is part of being human for a man and a woman to come together to form a family. This isn't an affectation of culture or politics or economics (the preeminence of the *nuclear family* is, but that's a topic for another chapter); it's built into our very nature.

Proponents of sexual liberation point to this or that species of animal in which mating results in no permanent bond and say, "Aha! Monogamous marriage is not 'natural' at all!" Such a response, though, gets the idea of the naturalness of marriage completely wrong. To say that an institution or behavior is "natural" for human persons does not mean simply that it "can be observed in the natural world." Then, anything would go. (It should be noted that these progressives never point to mantises, which practice sexual cannibalism—the consumption of the male by the female during mating—when finding animals whose sexual practices humans should mimic.)

Similarly, to say something is "natural" for human persons does not mean that the desire for that behavior can be commonly observed in society. We can desire any number of things, all the way from gluttony to murder, that fail to respect our distinctive humanity. Rather, when we say that marriage is a natural institution, we mean that it accords with our unique nature as human beings. This means that the behaviors of giraffes or dolphins or porcupines are irrelevant, as are our own disordered desires that we rationalize as irresistible instinct.

So, what *is* marriage as a natural institution for human beings? The traditional formulation used in Catholic marriage apologetics is that it has three essential attributes: permanence, exclusivity, and openness to life. Put most simply, these norms are essential to the total self-giving that is implied in human sexuality. If two people really do become "one flesh," then that bond cannot be severed, that comprehensive union cannot be shared with others, and that self-gift cannot be limited by artificially ruling out procreation.

In a letter quoted in Pope Pius XI's encyclical *Casti Connubii*, Pope Pius XI affirmed that the norms we associate with Christian marriage also inhere in natural marriage:

> Hence it is clear that marriage even in the state of
> nature, and certainly long before it was raised to
> the dignity of a sacrament, was divinely instituted

in such a way that it should carry with it a perpetual and indissoluble bond which cannot therefore be dissolved by any civil law. Therefore although the sacramental element may be absent from a marriage as is the case among unbelievers, still in such a marriage, inasmuch as it is a true marriage there must remain and indeed there does remain that perpetual bond which by divine right is so bound up with matrimony from its first institution that it is not subject to any civil power.[1]

Therefore, you don't need to affirm the Catholic faith (or any faith) to be able to understand or to contract a natural marriage. Marriage with all its norms and duties is part of being human, not just part of being Catholic.

But that's not the end of the story. Marriage is also a sacrament, and that truth brings new considerations to the table.

*   *   *

In a culture that enforces secularism in all public spheres, most of all in politics, it can be tempting to end the analysis with the natural elements of marriage. After all, the sacramental nature of marriage is not only religious, it's sectarian. Bringing the sacramental to the discussion accentuates the differences between the Catholic understanding of marriage and the minimalist public understanding.

---

[1] Pius XI, Encyclical Letter on Christian Marriage *Casti Connubii* (December 31, 1930), §34, quoting Pius VI, Official Reply to the Bishop of Agria *Rescript. ad Episc. Agriens* (July 11, 1789).

But the truth is that the natural and sacramental cannot be fully disentangled. When our Lord instituted the Sacrament of Matrimony, He didn't add a layer on top of natural marriage; it would be more accurate to say He *reinstated* and *perfected* natural marriage in all its challenge and splendor. Here's how Pius XI described the transformation of the original law of marriage into a sacrament:

> Therefore although before Christ the sublimeness and the severity of the primeval law was so tempered that Moses permitted to the chosen people of God on account of the hardness of their hearts that a bill of divorce might be given in certain circumstances, nevertheless, Christ, by virtue of His supreme legislative power, recalled this concession of greater liberty and restored the primeval law in its integrity by those words which must never be forgotten, "What God hath joined together let no man put asunder."[2]

Without the grace that flows from the Sacrament of Matrimony, even natural marriage was so hard that Moses was compelled to make exceptions. It is the sacrament that makes marriage possible, both personally and as the foundational social institution; it is the sacrament, therefore, that makes sustainable human societies possible.

And so while a couple who enters into a natural marriage without the benefit of the sacrament in most cases contracts a true marriage with all the duties that are implied, it is

---

[2] Ibid., §34.

like a football team without a coach—legitimate, but still missing the element that provides the order and support necessary for success.

The sacrament brings to bear the grace of God that is necessary to live out even the basic requirements of natural marriage. Quoting the Council of Trent, Pius XI eloquently explained what it means for marriage to be raised to the level of sacrament:

> For to Christians [sacrament] is not a meaningless and empty name. Christ the Lord, the Institutor and "Perfecter" of the holy sacraments, by raising the matrimony of His faithful to the dignity of a true sacrament of the New Law, made it a sign and source of that peculiar internal grace by which "it perfects natural love, it confirms an indissoluble union, and sanctifies both man and wife."[3]

Marriage may be a natural institution, and natural marriages may be real, but to exclude the sacramental is to exclude the grace that "perfects," "confirms," and "sanctifies." The purely natural understanding of marriage, therefore, is radically incomplete.

*　　*　　*

Tucked into the discussion of matrimonial consent in the Catechism of the Catholic Church is a beautiful and meaningful declaration about the nature of Christian marriage:

---

[3]　Ibid., §39, quoting Conc. Trid. Sess., XXIV.

"Sacramental marriage is a liturgical act . . . [that] introduces one into an ecclesial *order*" (1631; emphasis added). The word "order" is pregnant with meaning. The Catechism explains that the concept of an *order* comes from the Roman understanding of "an established civil body" (1537). In the Church, then, members of an order have specific prescribed responsibilities within the larger Body of Christ in the same way civil institutions have specific responsibilities within society. And this "ecclesial order" only exists within the Church and is senseless outside of it. The fullness of marriage, therefore, is safeguarded in and by the Church.

Further, the term for initiation into an order is *ordination*. To us moderns, *ordination* has come to mean only the initiation into the priesthood we call the Sacrament of Holy Orders, but matrimony is also, in fact, a kind of ordination—the initiation into the order of marriage.

And so when we say that the married couple presides over the "domestic church," that's not a mere analogy. The family is not *like a* church; it *is* a church over which parents have authority delegated to them by *the* Church. Similar to the way a parish priest has the souls of the faithful in his church entrusted to him, parents have the souls of their children entrusted to them.

This is a truly awesome responsibility, and it's not optional; it's part of what it means to be married. How can we possibly fulfill the ecclesial duties of the order of marriage in addition to all the other norms that are natural to the institution? That's why marriage is a sacrament: in the same way the grace conferred in Holy Orders gives young men the strength to fulfill the overwhelming spiritual and temporal duties of the priesthood, the grace conferred in matrimony gives couples the resources they need to succeed.

* * *

The Church has, over the years, developed several ways to describe the essence of marriage. In the early years of the Church, St. Augustine wrote about the three *goods* of marriage, which he identified as *proles*, *fides*, and *sacramentum*. These are aspects of marriage that are inherently good and that, in turn, redound to the good of the married couple.

Proles, from which we get the English word "prolific," refers to childbearing and childrearing—not just having children but educating them in the love of Jesus Christ. *Fides*, from which we get the English word "fidelity," refers to the faithfulness between the spouses—not just the lack of infidelity but the constant work of mutual self-giving. *Sacramentum*, from which (you guessed it) we get the English word "sacrament," refers to the sacramental grace that comes with matrimony—not just the one-time outpouring at the nuptial Mass, but the everyday relationship with Christ the couple cultivates.

Traditionally, the Church has also taught that there are three *ends* of marriage. These are best considered as the extrinsic goods to which marriage is ordered rather than the goods that emerge from within marriage.

The primary end of marriage, echoing Augustine, is bearing and bringing up children in the faith. The secondary end, shifting the focus (also following Augustine) from children to the married couple, is the mutual aid between the spouses, both in the practicalities of everyday life and in the hard work of holiness. The tertiary end of marriage, a bit less cheery but still important, is the *remedium concupiscentiae*—the relief of concupiscence, by which sexual urges are channeled in a way that honors God and human nature. In *Casti Connubii*, Pius XI adds another layer to the Church's understanding of marriage when he writes of the "chief reason" for the institution:

> This mutual molding of husband and wife, this determined effort to perfect each other, can in a very real sense . . . be said to be the chief reason and purpose of matrimony, provided matrimony be looked at not in the restricted sense as instituted for the proper conception and education of the child, but more widely as the blending of life as a whole and the mutual interchange and sharing thereof.[4]

Before this, the language of achieving perfection in this life was often reserved, especially in the minds of everyday Catholics, for the clergy and those in religious life. It was thought that only those states of life were suitable, in themselves, to prepare one for heaven. But here we see that not only is marriage a state of life—an ecclesial order—that can perfect us in holiness, but that mutual perfection of the spouses is the primary purpose of the sacrament.

*   *   *

---

[4] Ibid., §24.

Those inside and outside the Church who favor loosening the ancient norms of marriage often argue that those norms are so rigorous as to be impossible. These claims are buttressed by the ubiquity of divorce and otherwise shattered marriages, from American celebrities to British royals, and in every family and community. It seems that the only guarantee of marital success is good fortune.

The difficult truth is that these people are more right than they are wrong: without the benefit of the sacrament, even the norms of natural marriage are indeed impossible to fulfill. Further, in a culture utterly denuded of sacramentality, it is impossible to rebuild a culture of marriage.

This is not to say that everyone who marries without the Sacrament of Matrimony will become divorced or commit adultery or eschew children. It does mean, however, that only the grace of the sacrament can preserve marriage against the daily corrosion of lust and pride and selfishness. There's no standing still in our pursuit of holiness; we're either moving forward or backward. Only the outpouring of grace that comes with matrimony can sustain our momentum; without it, whether we realize it or not, we will slide inexorably away from God.

Those precepts of natural marriage—permanence, exclusivity, and openness to life—should not be considered as mere prohibitions. Marriage and holiness generally are about more than just avoiding pitfalls; they are about transforming ourselves into Christ. This is, remember, the "chief reason" for the institution. The marital examination of conscience can't just be in the negative; rather, it must accentuate our positive duties to advance in dedication (not just to avoid breakup), to grow in faithfulness (not just to avoid adultery), and to grow in the self-forgetfulness necessary to build a family where life is welcomed and nurtured (not just to avoid artificial contraception).

Lust, in particular, requires constant vigilance. While our exploitative popular culture doesn't make combatting lust any easier, we must not blame the culture for our struggles; the battle with lust occurs in the heart, not in complaining about "the culture." Sexual temptation wasn't invented by advertising agencies and movie producers; it's been with us since the Fall.

Remember the challenging words of Jesus: "You have heard that it was said, 'You shall not commit adultery.' But I say to you that every one who looks at a woman lustfully has already committed adultery with her in his heart" (Mt 5:26–28). When then-presidential-candidate Jimmy Carter confessed to "adultery in [his] heart" in an interview with *Playboy*, he was widely mocked, but this was a rare instance of a public figure taking seriously the biblical mandate of purity: it begins in the interior life before manifesting itself in the visible world.

The problem is that we don't want to believe that sacramental grace is *necessary* to living out marriage successfully. We want to believe that we can go it alone, and that while other (weaker) people might need help, our character can withstand the daily onslaught of the devil (who hates marriage precisely because of its sanctifying quality). And even if we accept the importance of sacramental grace, we might think of it as a kind of bonus that *improves* the experience of marriage rather than making it possible at all.

This may seem severe, even despairing, but in fact it's the opposite. Marriage may be exacting, but it's such a beautiful way of life. How wonderful that our Lord has given us this "perfecting" institution, and how much more wonderful that He has given us the grace to live it to the fullest!

And how wonderful that He gave us an example of a perfect marriage to serve as a model and an inspiration: the Holy Family.

The Perfect Marriage

E very parent has felt like a failure at some point—and some of us more often than others.

It's easy to take a romantic view of the Holy Family, as if they were angels rather than human beings. But even though Mary and Jesus never sinned, that doesn't mean there were no parental mistakes. And it doesn't mean Jesus never frustrated His earthly parents.

Jesus was twelve years old when He stayed behind in Jerusalem after the Passover observances. St. Luke records that Mary and Joseph had traveled an entire day before they realized their boy was missing. Any parent can relate to the fear, anxiety, and embarrassment Jesus' parents must have felt as they turned back toward Jerusalem (Lk 2:41–51).

But just imagine: Mary and Joseph felt like they had lost not just any teenager but *the Son of God*. This story is often used as an analogy for the experience of the Dark Night of the Soul, when one suddenly loses the confidence and consolation of the presence of the Lord. We wonder, as Jesus' parents must have wondered, if we have lost God or, more distressingly, if He has abandoned us. Even knowing in an intellectual way that God never abandons us often isn't enough to calm the anxiety that comes with feeling His absence so acutely.

And so we should not be surprised that the Blessed Mother's first words to her precious son, whom she has found only after three full days of searching, are ones of exasperation: "Son, why have you treated us so? Behold, your father and I have been looking for you anxiously." But the twelve-year-old Christ gently rebukes His mother with a rhetorical question: "How is it that you sought me? Did you not know that I must be in my Father's house?" (Lk 2:48–49).

Jesus' rebuke should sting us as it surely stung His parents, but it should also give us consolation for two reasons. First, even the sinless Blessed Mother did not always understand the ways of the Lord, and she felt the anxiety that comes with His apparent absence. How much more so should we sinners, therefore, expect to feel the pangs of abandonment when the Lord feels far away from us? Second, and more importantly, Jesus' response reminds us that we can always find Him in the temple—the temple of the Church where He rests in the tabernacle and the temple of our hearts where He rests, waiting patiently for us to seek Him out.

This is the key to understanding the Holy Family: studying Mary and Joseph always has a way of turning our focus to Jesus Christ. The primary community of which Jesus was a member—His family—didn't subsume or dilute His identity. Rather, His family accentuated His nature, both human and divine.

The Holy Family should serve as a reminder that our families should not become excuses for ignoring Jesus, but rather showcases that display His grace and love and truth more brilliantly than any individual can on his or her own. Jesus, like all of us, finds His fullness in community.

*   *   *

The Gospel of Matthew begins with a sentence fragment, perhaps intended as a title: "The book of the genealogy of Jesus Christ, the son of David, the son of Abraham" (Mt 1:1). You may recognize the genealogy from lectors tripping over names like "Ammin'adab" and "Zerub'babel" during Christmas Eve Mass. But this section is more than a list of funny names: it is the interpretive key for the entire New Testament.

The Greek word for "genealogy" is *geneseos*, which can also mean "beginning" or "origin." It's where we get words like "generation" and "genetics" from. It's also where we get the name for the first book of the Bible: Genesis. And so right off the bat, Matthew is telling his readers, who were familiar with the Jewish Scriptures, that Jesus Christ is a New Beginning not just for the Chosen People but for the entire world.

We call this section of the Scriptures the "New Testament," but the Greek word for "testament" can also mean "covenant." So Matthew isn't just announcing a new revelation from God, but a new covenantal relationship between the Lord and the world He created. In fact, it would be just as accurate—and more meaningful—to call the Gospels, Epistles, and Revelation the "New Covenant."

Notice that Matthew opens his book about this New Covenant with a list of family ties. The concepts of "covenant" and "family" are intrinsically related; covenant oaths, such as those used for marriages or adoptions, were the means of forging family relationships. In the New Covenant, we are all brought into a family relationship with the Lord. The Catechism of the Catholic Church puts it with characteristic concision: "The Church is nothing other than 'the family of God'" (1655).

*   *   *

It is through the Church and her sacraments (which take the form of covenant oaths) that we are brought into a family relationship with the triune God. How fitting, then, that "Christ *chose* to be born and grow up in the bosom of the holy family of Joseph and Mary" (CCC 1655; emphasis added). The familial nature of our relationship with Christ is modeled by the very circumstances of His earthly life.

Jesus could have burst onto the scene in any number of ways. He could have walked out of the wilderness as a fully-formed adult. He could have been raised in a royal court. He could have descended from heaven amid thunder, lightning, and fireworks. But in His perfect wisdom, He decided it would be most suitable to His nature and ours to be born like any other baby and raised by a carpenter and a common maiden.

We often adore the crèche with the thought, "What humility He showed, to be God and yet to be born into this!" This is a true and good sentiment, but we shouldn't let ourselves think that Jesus was born into a situation that somehow did not suit Him. The Holy Family—their poverty, their simplicity, their humility—*precisely* suited Him. It was in this perfect family that He demonstrated the way of living most proper for children of God.

In the same way, then, that the domestic church of the family is the first center of religious practice for young children, the domestic church of the Holy Family was the seed of the Church. We can even say that the Church is an extension of the Holy Family. Through Jesus Christ, Mary and Joseph were the first people to be brought into a family relationship with the Lord. Now, the Church is the universal expression of that family.

When we call fellow Christians "brothers and sisters in Christ," that's not a metaphor. We aren't saying (and shouldn't be thinking) that our siblings in Christ are only *facsimiles* of real brothers and sisters, or that we should treat them *as if* they were our brothers and sisters. No, we Christians truly share an adoptive Father in the Trinitarian God—the God of Abraham and of Moses, the God who took on our humanity in Jesus Christ. We are family—not by the blood of genetic inheritance, but by the blood of Jesus.

As the first family and the first church of the New Covenant, the Holy Family isn't just the model family community, but the model ecclesial community. Mary and Joseph show us what and who we can be when we unite ourselves to Christ.

*   *   *

There has never been and never will be a more perfect marriage or a more perfect church than the Nazarene trinity we call the Holy Family. Mary and Joseph were in constant contact with the Son of God; every interaction with Jesus was a kind of prayer. They submitted themselves to His divine will, while He humbly submitted Himself to their earthly authority in "the temporal image of his filial obedience to his Father in heaven" (CCC 532).

What an incredible responsibility—to have parental authority over the Son of God! While we must imagine this duty weighed on Jesus' mother and foster father, we also have every reason to believe they wore it lightly. After all, both (Mary especially) were imbued with tremendous grace at the Annunciation of Christ's coming, and then continually henceforth as they spent their lives in the physical, human presence of God.

But they still had to cooperate with this outpouring of grace. Like all of us, Jesus' family had free will. Despite Mary's Immaculate Conception, she didn't *have* to give her *fiat* to God through the angel Gabriel. Joseph didn't *have* to take on the potential scandal of wedding a pregnant virgin (who would believe that story?). They didn't *have to* stay on the path to Calvary when Simeon spoke to Mary during the presentation of Jesus in the temple, saying "a sword will pierce through your own soul" (Lk 2:35). And yet, every day for more than thirty years, they pressed forward to a culmination they knew would be painful, but not yet *how* painful.

The thought might come to mind, "If I saw and spoke with Jesus every day in my home, it'd be easy to be good! Mary and Joseph had the ultimate advantage in the quest for holiness." But that's just the thing: we *do* have the advantage of the presence of the Lord. We can appeal to Him every day, several times a day, just like His earthly parents could. We can make Him the centerpiece of family life. We can even, incredibly and beautifully, encounter His tangible and complete presence in the Eucharist, both in Communion and in adoration.

This takes some imagination, but more than that it takes trust—trust that He is there and that He is listening even when we can neither see nor hear Him. Again the Holy Family stands out as a model. Mary and Joseph had to trust Him too, even when it was nearly impossible to do so. They had to trust that His teenage excursion to the temple was God's will, not precocious rebellion. They had to trust that His departure for public ministry was not a rejection of their three decades of family life. And, most powerfully, they had to trust that His delivering Himself into the clutches of His bloodthirsty enemies would somehow be for the best.

We should not look at the Holy Family as some ethereal, unattainable goal, but as an example of what is truly possible when we make Jesus Christ the center of our lives. After all, this is the essence of the New Covenant: the extension of family ties with the Lord to all the world. The Holy Family shows us what that means. It's up to us to follow through.

*   *   *

The Holy Family is more than a part or an exemplar of the New Covenant. In a very real way Mary, Joseph, and Jesus are the earthly manifestation of the covenant itself. That is, the Holy Family isn't just (as I've said) the first church and the first family of the New Covenant: as *the* family of God, the Holy Family is *the* Church and *the* family in its essential perfection.

Through the ages, saints and scholars have referred to the Church as the "perfect society."[1] This might seem like an extravagant claim to any student of Church history or anyone who keeps up with current events. No one can deny that the Church has been devastated by scandal again and again. And yet that concept of the perfect society has always been used, even by people who are well acquainted with the human corruption that infects the Church's divine nature.

But the skeptic misses the point in two ways. First, the Church as perfect society refers not just to the visible Church here on earth (the Church Militant), but to the souls in purgatory (the Church Suffering) and the saints and angels in heaven (the Church Triumphant). Considered in its wholeness, the Church comprises the entire communion of saints, and is perfectly united with God as His spouse—and there's that family analogy again.

Second, to say that the Church is the perfect society is not to say that every member of the hierarchy or every Vatican decree is perfect; that would be mad. Rather, it means that the Church uniquely has the natural and supernatural resources *to perfect us*. The fact that many Catholics—even people who are tightly ensconced in the day-to-day goings-on of the Church—fail to take full advantage of these resources (most notably the sacraments) does not change the reality of the Church as a medium of God's perfecting grace.

The Holy Family, then, is this perfect society in min-

---

[1] See Scott Hahn, *Angels and Saints: A Biblical Guide to Friendship with God's Holy Ones* (New York: Image, 2014) on the perfection of the heavenly realm and how the Church manifests this perfection to us here on earth.

iature. All of the qualities of the Church—including her Militant, Suffering, and Triumphant blocs—were present in that humble Nazarene home. Everything we could ever hope for in this life, including everything we need to enjoy eternity in the next life, was contained in that one perfect family. The perfect marriage *is* the perfect church. The perfect church *is* the perfect society. And they all have Jesus Christ at the very center. It's hard to imagine claims that challenge modern, secular notions of politics and culture more than these. They explode all the assumptions we have about the divisions (arbitrary and artificial, it turns out) between the private and the public and between the religious realm and the political realm.

And yet there they are, implied right at the very beginning of the New Covenant—implied, that is, in the New Covenant itself. Grappling with the consequences of these claims will take up much of the rest of this book.

*   *   *

But before we move on, let's return to the temple in Jerusalem, where the twelve-year-old Jesus has been teaching the teachers. St. Luke tells us that after gently admonishing His mother and foster father for failing to check His "father's house" first as they searched for Him, "he went down with them and came to Nazareth, and was obedient to them; and his mother kept all these things in her heart" (Lk 2:51).

We all at some point or another have had a boss or an older sibling or even a bishop who, in our considered opinion, wasn't quite suited to the authority he or she had. And of course we grumble about how unfair it is and how we would *certainly* do a better job and so on. How petty this seems, though, in comparison with the cheerful obedience Jesus Christ gave to His human parents. How incredible! The Creator condescended to obey His creatures.

(St. Joseph features most starkly here: while Mary was uniquely sinless, her husband was not. He was a man blessed with extraordinary graces, but he was not perfect. And yet the Son of God obeyed His earthly father as he managed the household and trained his son in carpentry and surely made a few faux pas along the way.)

The Catechism tells us that "the everyday obedience of Jesus to Joseph and Mary both announced and anticipated the obedience of Holy Thursday" (532), when Jesus prayed in the garden of Gethsemane, "Father, if you are willing, remove this chalice from me; *nevertheless not my will, but yours, be done*" (Lk 22:42; emphasis added). Jesus' obedience to the proper *human* authority in the Holy Family "was the temporal image of his filial obedience to his Father in heaven" (CCC 532).

In the same way, our obedience to proper earthly authorities prepares us to be obedient to the Lord. But when this world's authorities go haywire, whether in the closeness of the family home or in faraway capital cities, our ability to practice that "filial obedience" is undermined. Worse, inasmuch as these authorities represent God's final authority, their dysfunction disfigures our vision of who our God really is.

Throughout history, the fate of the Church and of civil authorities have been particularly intertwined with the health of marriage as a public institution. It is in the family where we first encounter the paternal relationship that serves as our best earthly representation of our relationship with the Lord. When marriage suffers, so then does our view of that relationship and, by extension, our view of God Himself.

Marriage, church, society—these three concepts form an integrated whole. They rise and fall together. And any attempt to divide them results in a cascading disintegration that is all but impossible to arrest.

CHAPTER 6

A Tumultuous History

For centuries scholars have pondered how it was that the Church grew so quickly in the first few centuries after the death, Resurrection, and Ascension of its founder, Jesus Christ. On the one hand this is a ridiculous line of inquiry, at least for secular analysis: the answer is the inspiration of the Holy Spirit. But God works through the lives of particular people in particular places at particular times, and so we can still learn a great deal from historical-sociological analyses.

It turns out that there had always been a hint right under the noses of researchers and laymen alike. It was a subtle hint, hidden in plain sight in recurring language in the Acts of the Apostles that is easily skipped over in a quick reading. But once you see it, you can't stop noticing it: throughout the narrative of the first evangelists, we continually read that new Christians came into the Church not alone, *but with their entire families.*

In Macedonia, Paul, Silas, and Timothy converted a young woman named Lydia who "was baptized, *with her household*" (Acts 16:15; emphasis added). Later on in the Macedonian mission, after being freed from prison by an earthquake, Paul and Silas "spoke the word of the Lord to [the jailer] and *to all that were in his house. And he took them the same hour of the night, and washed their wounds, and he was baptized at once, with all his family*" (Acts 16:32–33; emphasis added). And then in Corinth, St. Paul's preaching convinced "Crispus, the ruler of the local synagogue, [who] believed in the Lord, *together with all his household*" (Acts 18:8; emphasis added).

There are more examples throughout the accounts of the early evangelists—enough that we can safely say that the baptism of entire families (including infants) was the norm. The Catechism of the Catholic Church asserts that "these families who became believers were islands of Christian life in an unbelieving world" (1655).

This is fitting from a theological point of view—the New Covenant brings us into a family relationship with God—but it also made sense sociologically. The evangelists were traversing a weakened and decadent Roman Empire marked by insecurity, instability, and immorality. The robustness of Christian teaching on marriage and family—especially with regard to the dignity of women—was a comforting balm for people accustomed to family breakdown. Men and women brought their families with them into the Church not just because of the family spirit of the movement, however, but more fundamentally because they wanted their families to be saved with them!

The conversion of kin contributed to the exponential growth of Christianity even amid the headwinds of persecution. How can we look around at our postmodern world, marked by decadence and dissipation that rivals Rome, and not wonder if the fullness of Church teaching on marriage might have the same effect?

*　　*　　*

While the truth of Jesus Christ is timeless, the precise way it is lived out differs from person to person, place to place, and age to age. Marriage is no exception. The nature of matrimony has not changed and cannot change, and yet marriage and family have taken many forms and served diverse social purposes across time and across cultures.

Scholars have described and accounted for these shifts in different ways. The nineteenth-century French thinker Frédéric Le Play drew a contrast between "patriarchal" and "stem" families, on the one hand, and "unstable" nuclear families on the other. The former, on his telling, were marked by continuity of duty and identity across several generations, whereas the nuclear family was more ephemeral and marked by regular breaking apart and building anew. The modern American sociologist Carle Zimmerman, in his classic *Family and Civilization*, preferred the terms "trustee family," "domestic family," and finally, in our time, "atomistic family." Zimmerman charted a consistent shrinking of the most important unit, from massive (and sometimes mythical) genealogies in the trustee family to households in the domestic family to individuals in the atomistic family.

These family structures, of course, correspond to shifts in the conception of marriage itself. Historian John Witte, Jr., for example, chronicles the secularization and privatization of marriage in his work *From Sacrament to*

Contract. The good-faith attempts by various Christian traditions to make marriage more *official* through canon and civil law made it vulnerable to capture by the individualist and secularist ideologies of the "Enlightenment" that swept through and continue to dominate civil institutions throughout the West.

The point is that while we have access to the timeless teachings of the Church, we are also acclimated to the particular ways marriage and family have been acted out in the contemporary West—and it is important that we do not confuse the two. Marriage has never been exactly as it is today, nor, of course, has it been as it was in ancient Israel or imperial Rome since those times. And yet, in Western history, marriage and family have never been unrecognizable—until, perhaps, this moment, when even the most enduring conventions, such as the necessity of opposite-sex couples, are being dismissed. The truth endures, however, even if it is obscured by sin and circumstance.

With that in mind, let's turn to the prevailing notion of family in ancient Israel and among the writers of Scripture: the clan.

*   *   *

It would not be an exaggeration to say that every aspect of life in ancient Israel revolved around the family. Family was the primary source of identity, authority, and responsibility for individuals and communities throughout the Old Testament and into the time of Christ.

Today if we were to list the layers of identity and authority in our lives, we might think geographically—neighborhood, city, region, nation—or politically—township, county, state, country—or perhaps even ecclesiastically—parish, diocese, Holy See. Few, if any, in the modern West would think primarily in terms of kinship, but this would have been the only concept to come to the mind of an ancient Israelite.

This structure, like a Russian nesting doll of family ties and duties, is demonstrated clearly in the Book of Joshua. The Lord reveals to Joshua that Israel's failure in battle can be attributed to the sins of a thief in their midst. Here is what God tells Joshua to tell the people about how He will identify the guilty party:

> In the morning therefore you shall be brought near by your tribes; and the tribe which the LORD takes shall come near by families; and the family which the LORD takes shall come near by households; and the household which the LORD takes shall come near man by man. (Josh 7:14)

Every individual had a household, which consisted of multiple generations living together. Every household was part of a family, which shared a common ancestor. And every family was part of a tribe, which descended from the twelve sons of Jacob in the Book of Genesis. This was the organizing principle of life. To be outside of this system—that is, to lack family ties—was to be, for all practical purposes, nobody at all.

Le Play would call this a patriarchal family, and Zimmerman would call it a trustee family system *par excellence*. In return for the structure and identity conferred by the clan, the individual was to be a caretaker of that legacy by fulfilling his familial duties without complaint. It is out of this system that the covenantal understanding of marriage emerged: joining families and creating new households were momentous but also harrowing events in the life of the community. The superstructure of the society depended on stable families and dutiful family members, and so it only made sense to beg God's blessing on new unions.

*   *   *

The differences between the prevailing form of marriage and family in the modern West and that of ancient Israel cannot be overemphasized. We live in the age of the "unstable" (Le Play), "atomistic" (Zimmerman) family. The form of family to which we are accustomed is the nuclear family, with two generations at most under one roof, but the cultural emphasis is clearly on the preeminence of the individual—personal rights rather than mutual responsibilities, contingent contracts rather than permanent covenants.

Despite the value-laden language of Zimmerman and especially Le Play, the nuclear family has much to recommend it. This family form, for instance, accentuates the importance of the parent-child relationship and allows more space for individual personality to flourish. The point here, however, is not to judge among the infinite variety of family systems, but simply to observe that different structures emerge under different circumstances—and that while each reflects certain truths about the nature of marriage and family, none can be said to be a universal ideal.

The nuclear family, for instance, is a conspicuously modern phenomenon. It is disputed whether it emerged from or simply had its preeminence confirmed by the Industrial Revolution, but there is no doubt that this family structure is related to modern economic structures. The constant churn of family households forming and breaking apart and re-forming and petering out is a perfect image of the creative destruction of capitalism.

Further, weakened family identities (to the extent we have "family identities" at all) usually go back no further than two, maybe three, generations—leaving more space for identity to be constructed through participation in the economy—through workplaces, consumer choices, and so forth. And fewer family duties allow employers to claim more of a person's time and labor from adolescence—and in many times and places, childhood—until old age.

And so the "traditional" model of familial perfection—an elegant mother and a diligent father and a few bouncing babies and maybe a rowdy golden retriever—is in fact contingent on the social, political, and economic circumstances of our time and place. Like the clannishness of ancient Israel, this model is a reflection just as much of historical circumstance as it is of enduring truths about marriage and family. It is essential to disentangle these considerations carefully; an authentically Christian conception of marriage and family must go beyond defending contemporary norms. Tradition goes much deeper than the 1950s—or even the Industrial Revolution and the civilization that emerged from it.

*   *   *

While the ancient Israelites lived in the presence of prophets and divinely inspired kings and we are limping along on the fumes of Christian civilization, we shouldn't automatically assume that the ancient family system is ideal or even superior to our own. Each model has lessons to learn from the other.

For instance, in ancient Israel *everything*—from inheritance rights to the application of justice—depended on one's place in the clan structure. This kind of total reliance on family ties is incompatible with principles of justice that are firmly established in Catholic social teaching, such as equality under the law and, indeed, the rule of law itself.

More than that, the dominance of family ties is incompatible with the New Covenant of Christ. In the Old Testament, the clan structure resulted in the common good being more or less completely circumscribed by kinship of blood. Duty to the clan superseded all other responsibilities—sometimes even those owed to God. But the baptized are now all joined by the kinship of Christ, and we recognize the universality of human dignity and its implications for justice. The twelve tribes of Israel were replaced by the Twelve Apostles who were dispatched to all peoples throughout the known world.

The ancient model overemphasized the transgenerational and communitarian aspects of family at the expense of both the common good of society and the good of the individual. Today we have overcorrected in favor of the individual and his or her nearest relations and at the expense of transgenerational and, again, society-wide solidarity.

The nuclear or atomistic family—marked by two-generation households that decay into one-generation households as children reach maturity—is associated with certain undeniable goods. The prosperity that correlates with the flexibility and dynamism of this family arrangement is apparent. Further, as I mentioned earlier, it recognizes and celebrates the primacy of the parent–child relationship— the building block and microcosm of society.

But dynamism comes at the cost of stability, and the inward focus of the nuclear family comes at the cost of solidarity. We can and should, therefore, admire and wish to emulate certain aspects of the biblical culture of marriage and family without adopting it wholesale (which would, in any case, be impossible in our times). The transgenerational identity and solidarity of the biblical family, for instance, not only has social benefits but reflects the truth of God's covenantal relationship with His people. In practice, this might mean embracing multigenerational households both to support the aging and to enrich the experience of youth—even if prevailing attitudes and structures make this challenging. Our first commitment must always be to seek out and live out what is *good*, not what is normal, respectable, or easy.

*   *   *

And so when I speak of marriage and family in this book, you should not just imagine the mid- to late-twentieth-century American suburban ideal. God's truth and Church teaching reach both further into the past and further into the future than any cultural trend or social norm or economic system. If our goal is to recapture an idyllic past, as I said at the very beginning of this book, we will always be disappointed.

Jesus Christ, His bride the Church, the dignity His Father gave to human beings: these endure well beyond any time frame we can imagine. Therefore, when we think about them, we must never feel constrained by what is customary—in our time or in any time. Yes, present norms have value as the products of accumulated reason and experience; but we must not be afraid to recognize when poorly formed reason and misleading experience have brought us away from the fixed point of God's truth.

Just as we should never feel comfortable when reading Jesus Christ's call to perfection, we should never feel comfortable when we consider the truth of what marriage, family, and human society *can be* and *ought to be*.

CHAPTER 7

The Catholic Social Vision

It has long been said that *The New Yorker* film critic Pauline Kael expressed her incredulity at the 1972 election of Richard Nixon by saying, "No one I know voted for him!" This isn't actually quite right, but the actual quotation demonstrates just as much cultural and political insularity: "I live in a rather special world. I don't know one person who voted for Nixon."

Kael's observation has been deployed for decades as an example of the insularity of American cultural elites. But the truth is that these days her observation rings true for more and more Americans whose social circles have enclosed around a narrow range of experiences and viewpoints.

It is, more than ever, nearly impossible for a professor or attorney to understand the experience and perspective of a plumber or mechanic—and vice versa. It's not just that these professions occupy different social strata—that has always been the case—rather, it's that these classes are drifting further and further apart culturally, politically, and even geographically.

These trends have been chronicled by the sociologist Charles Murray in his 2012 book titled, appropriately, *Coming Apart*. In order to eliminate the confounding variable of America's legacy of institutionalized racism, Murray focused his analysis just on white Americans. And what he found is an accelerating divergence between the cultures and experiences of middle-to-upper class versus working-class whites.

One of the primary areas Murray studied was norms and behavior with respect to marriage and childbearing. The financial and social stability of the upper echelons of our society, it turns out, are directly related to stronger marital norms—more marriages, fewer divorces, less out-of-wedlock childbearing, less single parenthood, and so on. Whether these norms are a cause or an effect of a broader stability is popular to debate (it's almost certainly a little of both), but what's indisputable is that more stable social cohorts have stronger marital practices.

This divergence, both within and across racial and ethnic lines, has made it more and more difficult to perceive common ground across social divides. Whether it's identity politics or ethnonationalism, so much of our political thinking and discourse has been about how we can ensure the success of some groups *at the expense* of others. The idea of a truly common good, which was always backgrounded in American politics, has nearly receded out of view entirely.

This is both a challenge and an opportunity for Catholics. The Church's social vision has always been based in a robust concept of the common good—both naturally and supernaturally. The atrophy of a politics of the common good throughout the Western world makes it more difficult to bring the concept into the mainstream conversation—but it also means we are surrounded by people yearning for a social vision that's truly moral and inclusive.

*   *   *

When we say the Nicene Creed at Mass, we profess faith in a church that is "one, holy, catholic, and apostolic." In these four "marks of the Church" we can see the foundation of the Catholic social vision—and the answers that a divided, secular world is looking for.

The Church is One. In a culture obsessed with having as many choices as possible (a billboard for a regional convenience store chain in my neck of the woods touts the company's drink offerings with the line, "Are 500 beverage options excessive? Yes."), the oneness of the Church offers a reprieve. A distinctive feature of our age is a deep-seated uncertainty that our consumeristic choosing is adding up, or could ever add up, to anything truly good and enduring. The Church, however, confidently asserts that she is *the* miraculous spouse of Jesus Christ, and that there is no other.

The Church's oneness is also an answer to a society deeply divided along political, social, economic, and ethnic lines. There is not a Republican church or a Democratic church, a rich church or a poor church, a white church or a black church. The Church is one because God is one. In His eyes and those of the Church, our diversity of experiences and cultures only enhances the beauty of what we share: the image of God and the ability to share eternal life with Him.

The Church is Holy. She is both sanctified and a means of sanctification for others. While secularists wallow in something between self-pity and perverse self-congratulation over the apparent meaninglessness of existence, the Church boldly claims that, unique among human institutions, she bridges the divide between the natural and the supernatural—the human and the divine.

Steeped in humanity but oriented toward eternity, the Church and her social vision take account of both natural and supernatural realities. In so doing, she gives us something no secular account of society can muster: a purpose that goes beyond serving oneself and one's in-group. That purpose is salvation.

The Church is Catholic. When we speak the word "catholic" in the context of the Creed, we are not naming a denomination or religious "brand name." Rather, we are using that word in its original meaning, which is "universal." We call the Church "catholic" not just because that's her name, but because she is universal, and that universality is so essential to her that it identifies her character.

The Church cuts across every social division we could possibly dream up. Therefore, her vision for society is and must continue to be radically inclusive—much more so than any progressive social plans that use "inclusivity" as a buzzword, then proceed to exclude anyone who disagrees with their definition of it. The claim inherent in the Church's catholicity—that there is a good common to *every* member of society, and that good rests in the Church—may be the most jarring to modern ears, but also the most important and appealing. Catholicity implies a solidarity that is conspicuously lacking in all our mainstream politics.

The Church is Apostolic. "Sustainability" is a popular concept these days—we want sustainable communities, sources of food and energy, and so on. But what could be more sustainable than the Church? She can trace two millennia of unbroken apostolic succession and is assured of being able to do so until Christ comes again.

The Church's apostolic nature adds another dimension to her comprehensiveness: time. She exists in the here and now, but also reaches backward and forward in a unity through time that is unique among human institutions. In so doing, she provides a more solid foundation for social order than any other organization or ideology ever could. The Church, therefore, is an answer to the modern despair over whether anything can be truly lasting.

*   *   *

Taken together, the four marks of the Church point to one fundamental truth: the common end of humanity—that is, the fundamental good for which we have all been created— is eternal communion with our Lord in heaven. While the social and political orders cannot save us, they must be constructed around this essential aspect of our humanity. The failure to create an order that is conducive to salvation is, in a real sense, inhuman.

There is a tension here between the social and the individual aspects of salvation. Can we even speak of a contribution of the political order to the saving of souls if salvation (or damnation) is individualized? (That is, our eternal fate is determined person-by-person, not due to our affiliation with any group.) It seems that the safest political order might embrace a thoroughgoing liberalism, even libertarianism, that gives the *individual* as much latitude as possible to grow in relationship with the Lord.

This approach, however, resolves the individual/communal tension simply by obliterating the notion of communal responsibility—or, more precisely, by reformulating those responsibilities as purely personal choices. The premise calls to mind that famous passage in C. S. Lewis' *The Abolition of Man*:

> In a sort of ghastly simplicity we remove the organ and demand the function. We make men without chests and expect of them virtue and enterprise. We laugh at honour and are shocked to find traitors in our midst. We castrate and bid the geldings be fruitful.

The individualistic social order removes any notion of the common good from politics, then begs individuals to act independently for the good of others and the community at large. This is like slicing a runner's Achilles tendon and then urging him to sprint.

In truth, both our duty to love others and human nature itself demand that the notion of the common good be part of the structure of political order, not just a vain exhortation to individuals. If the second greatest commandment—"You shall love your neighbor as yourself" (Mt 22:39)—means anything at all, it means that we are to value the good of others no less than we value our own good. This means that we must do more than just act independently for the *private* good of ourselves and those closest to us; we must work to

THE CATHOLIC SOCIAL VISION

form a society ordered to the common good of all. Remember that when the lawyer challenged Jesus by asking, "And who is my neighbor?" He responded with the parable of the Good Samaritan (Lk 10:25–37).

The late and eminent St. Thomas Aquinas scholar Charles De Koninck pointed out in his *On the Primacy of the Common Good* that in the same way that our love of particular persons proceeds from our love of God, our love for particular goods—that is, the good of particular persons and communities—proceeds from our love for greater, more universal goods. God is Himself the universal good of all creation, and we therefore love this good most of all. This means, then, that we are to love and to pursue the common good of society more than any particular good, because those particular goods proceed from the common good.

*   *   *

What does all this business about the "common good" really mean, though? Is it the "greatest good for the greatest number" that we associate with utilitarianism? Is it the collectivism that we associate with Marxism? Is it the imposition of the state that we associate with fascism? Surely, you might be thinking, the Catholic social vision can't be associated with any of these!

And you'd be right! The common good is neither the aggregation of private goods that utilitarianism envisions, nor the strict equality of circumstances that Marxism is popularly seen to envision, nor the external good (De Koninck calls it an "alien good") imposed by some outside force that fascism envisions. But the fact that the notion of the common good has been abused doesn't mean we should abandon the concept ourselves; to the contrary, that makes it more important than ever to witness to the authentic common good.

Following De Koninck, the common good is neither *just* the good of the community as a whole (which might be in opposition to the good of individual members) nor *just* the collection of the private goods of every individual member of the community (which might be in opposition to the good of the community). Rather, the common good includes *both* the good of the community as a whole *and* the good of each member—and because it is by its nature inclusive and other-regarding, it is *greater* than the private good of any individual. The common good distinguishes itself by its *communicability*: it can be shared person-to-person and thus is ordered to *communion*, the selfless sharing of life for which God made us.

Echoing St. Thomas, De Koninck writes, "The good is what all things desire insofar as they desire their perfection." When we choose to follow the Lord rather than to sin, we aren't just choosing "the good" in some abstract way; we are choosing in a real and concrete way to enhance our perfection—to take a step toward the ultimate purpose of our existence, which is the perfection of eternal communion with the Lord. The perfection of the whole both *is constituted by* and *enhances* the perfection of the parts. No matter how different they may seem, the proper functioning of the liver is not distinct from the good of the pinky finger; they share a good—a "perfection"—in the good health of the entire body in which both participate and from which both benefit.

Another important aspect of the common good is that it is not diminished by anyone's participation in it. To use the bodily analogy again, in the same way that the pinky is not diminished by the good health of the liver, my ability to participate in the common good is not diminished by my neighbor's participation. This can be considered by analogy to the universal good of God Himself, which is "superabundant"—utterly inexhaustible. After all, every sort of perfection is a participation in God's eternal and all-encompassing being.

*   *   *

This all may seem abstract and maybe a little confusing. But it's important that we get the theoretical parts right; as I mentioned, the idea of the "common good" has been weaponized by many dangerous ideologies. If we're going to use the term, we must understand it so that we can use it properly.

Moving forward, I will flesh out what the common good looks like in practice rather than just in theory. Let's begin by observing that different communities have different common goods, and therefore different duties, associated with them.

The national community, for instance, has different goods and duties associated with it than the family community does. Due to the interconnected nature of economic systems, distributive justice—the ensuring that the resources of the community are equitably distributed among the people, including among those who are less able to participate in the economy—is associated with national (and even international) society; it would be senseless to saddle the family with such a duty. On the other hand, the education of children is proper to the family in a way that it is not to larger political communities, except in a supporting role.

More prosaically, consider the division of labor after a snowstorm. The local government salts and plows public roads because transportation infrastructure is a common resource that demands uniform treatment. If every resident were responsible for his own patch of roadway, the streets would be a patchwork of slippery messes. On the other hand, the shoveling of driveways and walkways is proper to households—with support from the wider community for the elderly and infirm—because the use of those resources is limited to the family and their guests.

These levels of authority, responsibility, and common good, taken together, are what the Church calls "subsidiarity." This aspect of Catholic social teaching is fulfilled when communities perform the duties that are proper to them, without encroaching on authorities above or below their own. It is often assumed that subsidiarity means that social problems should be solved at the *lowest possible* level, but this isn't quite right. It's more about which duties are *proper* to which communities than artificially imposing duties on smaller communities rather than larger.

* * *

In the Catholic social vision, the family remains the fundamental community and the model for all other communities. While all social goods flow from the universal good of God Himself, all social forms flow from the universal form of the family, which is itself an image of the Trinitarian form of God.

The family is a universal hermeneutic—that is, an interpretive key that is accessible to everyone—for thinking about and understanding human societies. Despite the wide range of differences in family traditions and structures, no matter what culture you come from—Eastern or Western, secular or religious, cosmopolitan or tribal—the concept of a mother, father, and children is recognizable and comprehensible. It is written into our nature.

We should look at the wider communities of which we are a part—even nationally and internationally—with a familial gaze. It is true, of course, that we don't have the same duties to a peasant in Malaysia or to a craftsman in Zurich or to a surfer in Malibu as we do to our nearest family. And yet all of these people share, in some form or another, in the universal reality of family, both earthly and heavenly. We have something in common with them that we have with no other creature, even the angels. They are, with us, part of the family of God instituted by the New Covenant.

The preeminence of family in the Catholic social vision implies another important requirement: the social order—including and especially the *economic* order—must be organized around the good of the communities that make up society, especially the family. This is both an extension of the "primacy of the common good" articulated by De Koninck and a statement of the special importance of the family relationship to a flourishing and sustainable human society.

We often speak of economics, in particular, as a kind of natural science around which we must organize family life, like the tides or the weather. This gets things exactly wrong. The family is the fundamental and natural principle of social order, and we must organize the economy around its needs. An economy in which duties to the marketplace interfere with duties to the family (including the necessity of leisure for recreation, religious instruction, and so on) is gravely disordered.

At the same time, the proper functioning of family life supports the liberty of political and economic life—essential components of the common good. A society that gets marriage wrong will not remain free for long: the family is the training ground for the virtues that make free societies possible. Consider especially the necessity of trust in economic relationships. Trust cannot be manufactured or purchased; it must be taught in the crucible of family life and then earned in interactions with the wider world. Without a well-functioning culture of marriage, the reliability of interpersonal trust decays, and thus the ability of economic life to proceed without stifling interference is crippled.

*   *   *

The good of the family and the common good of society cannot be separated; a society that would pursue one at the expense of the other is doomed to lose both.

And that's exactly what's happened throughout the Western world. We live in a society that is deeply suspicious of anything truly common—especially a common good in which we all share. Whatever vestigial understanding of the common good we might have had has been subsumed by competing ideologies and factions and identity groups all jockeying for power.

We can understand, however, why this might be: the common good makes claims on our choices and actions that are deeply uncomfortable, especially in a culture that values individual liberty and autonomy above all else. Nowhere is this truer than in the realm of sexuality. If the good of the family is essential to the common good of society, then so is the health of our marriage culture. And if marriage is essential to the common good, then so is a virtuous and ordered sexuality.

CHAPTER 8

Sex and the Common Good

One night in the eighties, I was driving along the beltway outside Washington, DC, and listening to Dr. Ruth Westheimer on the radio. Dr. Ruth, you may remember, burst onto the scene in the early 1980s with a nationally syndicated talk show in which she candidly answered listeners' questions about sex. She later expanded her shtick to television, becoming a trailblazer in normalizing the frank discussion of sex in the media.

More than anything else, though, Dr. Ruth is remembered for her thick German accent that gave listeners and viewers a clinical and humorous distance from the titillating content of her programs. And that was me on that late-night road trip, sampling the wares of our coarsening culture with (I told myself) an ironic distance that shielded me from being corrupted. Plus, what could be better for keeping me awake than listening to an old German Jewish woman talk about sex on the radio?

That night the charming Dr. Ruth took a call from a teenage boy—fifteen years old—who wanted to discuss his sexual relationship with his fourteen-year-old girlfriend. I was so taken aback by her reply that I couldn't continue to listen, and I never tuned in again: "Did you practice safe sex?" That was it. That was her first and primary concern—not their maturity, their emotional state, or their future, but just whether the sex was appropriately sterile. When the boy answered in the affirmative, she praised him and wished the couple well in their sexual exploration.

The first concept that came to mind as I turned off the radio was "desecration." The word "desecrate" is a shortening of "de-consecrate"; "consecrate," in turn, emerges from the Latin word *sacer*, or "sacred." To desecrate, then, is to take something sacred and treat it profanely, to take something dedicated to the Lord and treat it as merely one good among many.

Dr. Ruth's flippant response to that teenage boy was an incitement to desecration. She treated the sacred intimacy of sexual intercourse—and an especially harrowing example of that intimacy, since she was speaking to a teenager—as if it were a game of racquetball: her only concern was whether the participants wore proper safety equipment. What a pitiful downgrade of the sacredness of sex to the level of mere recreation!

Keep in mind that at that point I was not yet Catholic, and Protestants as a rule don't object to artificial contraception as such. And yet I knew that this laser focus on the sterility of sex to the exclusion of all other concerns was deeply disordered. I would later come to understand how the assumption that sex is and ought to be sterile—an assumption that emerges naturally from separating sex and procreation—provides the foundation for many other errors in thinking about sex, both personally and politically.

*   *   *

Sexual intercourse is simultaneously one of the most intensely private and intrinsically public actions we can perform with our bodies. The first claim is obvious enough, but the second is, to modern ears, like claiming the oceans are filled with mayonnaise. But this is only because we've been trained to think of procreation as a kind of bonus we can *choose* to add on to sex—like upgrading to first class—rather than being inherently part of human sexuality.

The modern view is that sex is inherently sterile and only becomes procreative by accident or by the choice of the participants. Therefore, we speak of contraception *failure* rates and *unplanned* pregnancies; sterility is, we assume, our natural state, while fertility is a choice or a mistake. This way of thinking is only possible, of course, due to the ubiquity of artificial contraception.

The Church has taught from the very beginning that just as human beings are made *for* something outside of ourselves—namely, communion with God—sex is made *for* something outside of its own enjoyment—namely, participation with God in the creation of new persons. This is not to say that sex is *only* for procreation, but that its *primary* end is procreation. This eternal teaching was vigorously reaffirmed both in *Casti Connubii* and, several decades later, in Pope Paul VI's famous *Humanae Vitae* (1968). The unity of the spouses is another good that comes from sex, but that unity is dependent on openness to the complete fruition of sex in forming a new life.

Sex is therefore *both* deeply intimate *and* ordered toward something (and, often enough, *someone*) outside of itself. We close the bedroom door to preserve that intimacy, but we cannot shut out the public nature of procreation. It is, to the modern mind, a paradox. But that's a problem with the modern mind, not with the nature of sex.

*   *   *

The truth about the nature of sex complicates our assumptions about private versus public spheres of life. The modern view is that the decisions, actions, and experiences of individual persons can be neatly divided between those two spheres. The division can be discerned with the question: Will this action appreciably affect the lives of others not participating in the action? So, my peanut butter brand preferences are private; but if I were to start a peanut butter company, my business decisions would be public.

The trouble with this distinction is that it pretends to be neutral, but in fact it's totally subjective—subject to prevailing forces of politics, culture, ideology, and so on. Some cultures, for instance, have developed elaborate rituals around a married couple's first night together; these rituals preserve the intimacy of the act of consummation itself, but recognize that there's an inescapably public interest in what happens behind those closed doors. In our privacy-obsessed culture, meanwhile, more and more parts of life are actually taking on a public valence, as businesses and individuals are hounded for failing to properly respect new concepts of gender and sexuality; whether a florist's conscience will permit her to arrange flowers for a same-sex ceremony is now said to be of utmost public importance.

This trend toward expanding the public at the expense of the private is frightening to many—especially religious persons who recognize that the powers-that-be seem intent on bringing all religious practice under the purview of a hostile public authority. This fear is well-founded, but the truth of the matter is a bit more challenging: our culture isn't wrong to recognize that moral actions have an inherently public dimension; it's just committed to enforcing a disordered morality.

There is no such thing as a "private vice." All sin is, to some degree or another, public. First, the well-being of individual souls is, in and of itself, part of the common good. Second, well-ordered souls contribute to the well-being, comprehensively understood, of those around them. A virtuous man will make it easier for his wife, children, friends, colleagues, and so on to pursue goodness for themselves. This doesn't mean that the public authority—the state—should punish every sin and vice; pursuit of the common good requires prudence. St. Thomas Aquinas famously argued that the common good might require that certain vices be permitted because trying to stamp them out would do more harm than good. But it does mean that so-called private moral decisions are not, properly speaking, outside the purview of public authority.

One of the reasons, therefore, that secular moderns recoil at the idea that sex and babies are intrinsically connected is that this fact has uncomfortable political consequences.

But what could possibly be of more public importance than the creation of new human beings—human beings who become, at the moment of conception, participants in the common good?

*   *   *

Throughout law and culture, we can find instances of the recognition that sex is unique among human activities. For instance, we know intuitively that sexual assaults are especially serious violations of another person, and this is reflected in laws that treat rape much more harshly than a punch in the nose. Sexually explicit content in television shows and movies, while increasingly common, has always been considered a special category when determining ratings and appropriateness for prime-time broadcasting. And now it is in vogue to build entire identities around sexual preferences—identities that everyone else must respect on pain of public shaming and ostracism. The list could go on: at some level, we know sex is unique.

And yet the dominant way of thinking about the actual act of sex in our culture is as a special kind of recreation—more athletic than spiritual, more concerned with personal enjoyment than interpersonal communion. (Marriage, on this account, is reduced from a godly covenant to a kind of revocable sex license.) We can see shadows of the truth all around us, but we can't bear the implications of that truth—that sex is terribly important not just to our self-understanding and self-fulfillment, but to the ongoing life of the community as a whole. We'll look at just two of the many ways sex is truly unique among human actions.

First, by virtue of being ordered toward procreation, sex is the one thing we do with our bodies in the order of nature that is most uniquely connected with the common good. "In the order of nature" is an important qualifier here. We perform many actions with our bodies such as prayer, worship, and liturgy that are oriented vertically, upwards to heaven, and that are directly related to the common good. These actions are truly essential to the thriving of any community. But horizontally—person-to-person rather than person-to-God—there is no bodily activity that pertains to the common good in the way sex does because of its orientation toward procreation.

Second, there is virtually nothing we do *exteriorly* in the order of nature that makes us more like God than sex. *Interiorly*, we participate in God's nature by reasoning and contemplating. And again, in the supernatural order there are innumerable actions we can perform that contribute to our divinization—our becoming like God. This is what it means to grow in holiness, and it is the ultimate purpose of the sacraments. This is the order of grace. But exteriorly in the order of nature, nothing reflects the Trinity in the same way as marital love and intimacy, where the two persons "become one flesh" (Gen 2:24; Mk 10:8) and, God willing, a third person issues forth and embodies that communion.

*   *   *

What does it mean for politics to say that nothing impacts the common good quite like sex does? It might be tempting to shunt this question aside by thinking that the common good is just an abstract principle, and that the relationship of sex to that concept is so complicated that it's impossible to figure out. That's basically the modern view: the common good is a nice idea and makes for compelling rhetoric, but it's way too abstract to actually apply to the way our government and our society function. This collapses into an individualistic relativism: everyone should just pursue the common good as they see fit.

While we are all called to act for the common good of our communities and society, our responsibility does not end there. If the *common* good is to mean anything at all, it must be a *common* project. In the traditional Catholic understanding, in fact, the common good is the primary purpose and aim of civil government.

The public authority is the means by which the community—as a community and not just a collection of individuals—pursues the goods that are proper to the community. This is what is meant by the term "subsidiarity" in Catholic social teaching: each level of society is to fulfill the duties proper to it. Higher levels of authority shouldn't meddle in the affairs of lower levels, nor should lower levels of authority try to tackle problems whose scope is beyond their competency. In the American context, we would say that the federal government shouldn't direct trash pickup in Peoria, and the Louisville city council shouldn't be *solely* responsible for services to the poor since distributive justice is a problem that is regional and national in scope.

If it is in the nature of the civil authority to pursue the common good, and if it is in the nature of sex that it uniquely pertains to the common good, then it is entirely within the purview of the state to regulate sex. More than that: any government that takes the common good seriously will take an interest in sexual behavior—and not just grave violations such as assault.

This doesn't mean, as I've said previously, that every sexual sin listed in the Catechism of the Catholic Church should be punished with jail time. Different circumstances demand different approaches, and very often criminalization creates more problems than it solves. The key understanding, though, is this: a state might choose not to criminalize sexual sin not because there is some value in the sin or in the freedom to commit it (there is never a right to sin), but because enforcement of a criminal statute would lead to greater evils.

The common good demands not that every bad thing be forbidden, but that the law facilitate virtue. This should be the primary consideration of any law or regulation: will this make it easier or harder for people to be good? Individual and communal virtue require a certain amount of freedom to be authentic, but when freedom surpasses goodness as the primary purpose of the civil authority, then God has been usurped by the whims of His creatures.

*   *   *

Getting sex wrong, as a matter of philosophy and as a matter of policy, is both a symptom and a cause of social breakdown. I have already spent an entire chapter outlining what happens when a society lets its culture of marriage wither—the collapse of solidarity, the growth of the state and the market as replacements, and the unease that comes with the dissolution of natural human relationships. Individualism is an unstable foundation on which to build a social order; it is a denial of our interdependent human nature, which emerges from the Trinity in whose image we have been formed.

But this then becomes a feedback loop: the culture teaches individualistic lessons to its young people, who in turn usher in an even more individualistic future. The 1960s and 70s brought no-fault divorce; the children of that era, having learned a purely individualistic and contract-based view of marriage, brought us same-sex marriage. When we misunderstand what sex and marriage are *for*, we misunderstand what human beings are *for* (and vice versa). The errors compound one another.

Many well-meaning observers argue that the safest and best course is for the state, as far as possible, to maintain a hands-off approach to sex and marriage. Allow individuals to define and live out these concepts as they will, the argument goes, but the state should remain neutral. Even if the consequences of disordered and sinful behaviors are never fully private, maybe it's safer to pretend as if they were rather than trust the state to get it right. And if people mess it up, well, that's on them.

This libertarian approach is inadequate, though, because it cannot account for the common good. We are forbidden to be indifferent to the fate of our neighbor. And while we have different duties to the neighbor across the street than to the neighbor across the country, the civil authority is an essential means—though certainly not the only means—by which we pursue the common good of *everyone* in society, even if in an attenuated way.

We cannot wash our hands of our Christian duty to the common good by appealing to freedom because we can observe the predictable consequences of freedom. Again, this doesn't mean that freedom isn't good; freedom is a necessary condition of the common good. But freedom does not constitute the common good all by itself. Embracing the mantra of "freedom" in sex and marriage has resulted in (to name just a few consequences) an explosion in broken families, the normalization of pornography, the acceptance of all manner of disordered actions and desires, and an intense feeling of alienation and loneliness that pervades especially younger and poorer communities.

In the Gospel of Matthew, Pontius Pilate couldn't bring himself to condemn the Lord to crucifixion because he knew it was wrong. So instead, Pilate asked the mob if they would like him to release Jesus or Barabbas, knowing what its answer would be. When he pressed the crowd once more, he was rebuked further: "Let him be crucified."

> So when Pilate saw that he was gaining nothing, but rather that a riot was beginning, he took water and washed his hands before the crowd, saying, "I am innocent of this righteous man's blood; see to it yourselves." (Mt 27:24)

We cannot try to wash our hands of our duty by appealing to the crowd like Pontius Pilate. If we know that unmitigated freedom will descend into slavery—whether the subjugation of the weak to the strong, or the subjugation of the person to sin—then we cannot embrace that freedom and pretend that we have not made the decision to condemn.

*   *   *

There is no neutrality between good and evil—not for us, and not for the state. Every law, regulation, and policy, whether regarding barbershop quartets or abortion, includes a moral judgment or assumption about what is good for society. There is no way to craft a law that doesn't impose morality in some way or another.

A government that pretends to remain neutral with regard to competing views of sex instead endorses the prevailing norms. In the case of the modern West, that means individualism and libertinism, concepts that naturally favor the powerful—those who can better afford the economic costs of family breakdown and social isolation. Children, the poor, and the unborn are all dispensable afterthoughts.

The stability that comes with solid marriages and ordered sexuality is essential to coping with the natural unpredictability of our lives. To dismiss that stability in favor of a false liberation is to embrace a precariousness that will increasingly leave behind broken persons, families, and communities. The common good demands a civil authority that takes this seriously. If this is unthinkable in a modern and liberal society, that is a problem with modernity and liberalism, not with the Church's view of sex and the common good.

CHAPTER 9

Apocalypse and Society

In the twentieth century we perfected the means to split two things that had previously seemed indivisible: the atom and the family. Both developments have had social and political consequences heretofore unimaginable. What we didn't realize is that the forces unleashed in the splitting of the atom would be more easily contained than those unleashed by the splitting of the family.

Atom-splitting has ushered in an apocalyptic era—that is, an era in which the utter and efficient annihilation of humanity is within humanity's power. This has led to a certain fascination with apocalypses (or *the* Apocalypse), whether the "mutually assured destruction" satirized in *Dr. Strangelove* or the world-ending disasters portrayed in *Armageddon* or *The Day After Tomorrow* or zombie flicks.

The real apocalypse includes less adventure but infinitely more power and awe. The word comes to us from the Greek title of the last book of the Bible—*apokalypsis*—which is usually rendered as "revelation." The Catholic Edition of the Revised Standard Version of the Bible, for instance, calls the book "The Revelation to John" with "The Apocalypse" in parentheses. (The "John" to whom these visions occurred is known to Scripture scholars as the mysterious "John of Patmos" and in the tradition as John the Evangelist.)

Calling the book "Revelation" makes clear that *apokalypsis* does not actually refer directly to destruction, as it has come to mean in modern usage. Rather, the apocalypse is a revelation—a revealing—of God's will for the world and, at the end of time, of God Himself to all His creatures. With this final revelation comes the destruction of the world; hence our association of apocalypse with annihilation.

This is, however, only part of the story. Apocalypses, in the basic sense of the word, happen every day—little revelations of God's will that force us to adjust our plans or that even turn our lives upside down. In fact, every Mass is a little apocalypse, as God is revealed to us in the form of the Eucharist.[1] But there is also a deeper meaning to *apokalypsis* that goes beyond simple revelation: An apocalypse is an *unveiling*.

*   *   *

While the ancient Greek *apokalypsis* contains the concept of "revelation," in its fullness it means "unveiling." In fact, in the Jewish world at the time of the writing of the Book of Revelation, you would have been more likely to hear *apokalypsis* used at a wedding than in a description of the end of the world. That's because part of the week-long Jewish

---

[1] See Scott Hahn, *The Lamb's Supper: The Mass as Heaven on Earth* (New York: Doubleday, 1999), especially Part Three.

wedding festivities was the groom's lifting the veil of his bride.

In Jewish custom, this unveiling—this *apokalypsis*—took place just before the marriage was consummated. And so the unveiling revealed more than just a smiling face; it revealed the possibility of new life itself—the transformation from sterility to fertility, and the creation of a new family. Remember that for ancient Israelites, family was everything; politics and economics, identity and culture, history and future—everything was understood by reference to the fundamental reality of the clan. And so the wedding *apokalypsis* revealed both the expansion of the clan and the creation of a new family within the clan, a truly momentous and powerful occasion sealed in the loving intimacy of sexual union.

We might contrast this understanding of veiling, in which the veiled is revered, with the use of veiling as a symbol for ownership and subjugation, as is practiced in some cultures. It is a characteristic modern error to conflate all kinds and meanings of veiling into the latter, but this totally misunderstands the nature of veiling in traditional Jewish and Christian practice. That which is behind the veil is pure and powerful, not tarnished and possessed.

*   *   *

Not every unveiling is as momentous as the revealing of Christ's presence in the Mass—or even the radiant smiles shared between bride and groom on the altar. We encounter little apocalypses every day. The unchanging will of God is revealed to us on a regular and ongoing basis in the experiences—especially the unexpected experiences—of our lives. Sometimes these surprises are damaging in the popular sense of "apocalypse," such as the loss of a job or an adverse diagnosis. But even when they aren't obviously harmful, they always upend our plans and force us to reorient our lives. Marriage and family life are full of these apocalypses.

The most obvious unveiling of God's will in marriage is, of course, the creation of new life. It is popular these days to distinguish between "planned" and "unplanned" pregnancies, but this is nothing more than erasing God and replacing Him with our own will. (It's also biologically ignorant; while we can play the percentages such that conception is extremely unlikely, it's impossible to *ensure* conception.) At the end of the day, we need God's cooperation to create new life—even when we try to play God in the fertility lab.

No child can ever be truly planned or unplanned, and every child upends our expectations in some way or another. Even when we think we're ready—even when we've been preparing for parenthood for years—the reality always surprises us in some way or another. Maybe the ultrasound technician got it wrong and that pink nursery has to be painted blue. Maybe the genetic panel was faulty and the expected medical intervention won't be necessary. And maybe the doctor missed a serious problem that will require a lifetime of care, attention, and bill payments.

Children aren't the only source of little apocalypses in a family's life, of course. There are happy surprises, like raises and finding new friends, which give us new opportunities for spiritual, social, and intellectual growth. And there are unfortunate surprises, like illnesses and accidents, which challenge families and require them to divert emotional and financial resources away from leisure and luxuries and even perceived necessities to more pressing concerns.

Each of these moments reminds us that we are not and can never be totally in control. Just as the *apokalypsis* at the end of time will reveal Jesus Christ as King of Heaven and Earth, so should these little apocalypses remind us that He is the King here and now. We experience neither success nor failure, neither triumph nor tragedy, without Him.

Zooming out, we can therefore see that any social order that relies solely on human planning and expectations is bound for an apocalypse, little or big, sooner or later.

*   *   *

Our liberal, individualistic culture values autonomy above all else. It is assumed that the purpose of politics is to remove, as far as possible, limitations on individuals' choices, actions, and self-identifications. Any encumbrances on our autonomy must be freely chosen; that is, they must be *expressions* of our autonomy.

This lust for autonomy is simply the lust for control over all aspects of our lives—a control that requires power over other people's lives. This is nothing more or less than the first sin of Adam and Eve: the desire, as the serpent hissed to Eve, to "be like God" (Gen 3:5). It is the primordial temptation, the one that first separated us from God and that has plagued us ever since. Modern secular society has institutionalized this sin by erasing God and replacing Him with the will-to-power. Thus we also erase the common good: all our relationships and interactions become ordered to personal fulfillment rather than communal well-being.

But this project can never succeed. Autonomy and control require predictability. And so in both the public and private sectors, we spend billions and billions of dollars on "big data" and cybersecurity and surveillance in order to make life as safe and predictable and orderly as possible. We automate our homes, our cars, and our purchases. We convince women to cram as many artificial hormones as possible into their bodies to prevent the creation of new life. Every probability is plotted; every danger is identified; every contingency is planned for. The lust for autonomy ironically requires the radical centralization of power and authority.

But then *apokalypsis* strikes—and we're all the more upset about it because we had convinced ourselves we had everything figured out. And so rather than raising our eyes to heaven to ask for strength and wisdom and understanding to cope with this revelation of His will, we turn our eyes downward in dejection and despair. Remember the reaction of Adam and Eve when the Lord comes to see them after their disobedience: "the man and his wife hid themselves from the presence of the Lord God among the trees of the garden" (Gen 3:8). Once we turn from Him, our next self-destructive instinct is to run further away.

The lust for autonomy and control degrades into fear and despair. The antidote is trust in the loving and merciful God who has ordained every moment and movement since the beginning of time—not bureaucracies or data centers, which are mere man-made approximations, modern and secular towers of Babel by which we try to achieve omniscience. There will always be little apocalypses that surprise and challenge us; we find stability not in trying to eliminate them—a fool's errand—but in anchoring ourselves to the only changeless Being in the universe.

*   *   *

If this is true for individuals, then it is true all the more for societies. Liberal individualism cannot account for *apokalypsis* because it cannot account for any forces beyond human desire, will, and reason (usually in that order). And so liberal individualism is inherently unstable, hocking the snake oil of autonomy to people despairing not of a lack of freedom, but of a lack of meaning—a meaning that can only come from something that transcends themselves.

Erasing God eliminates the entire reason for political community to begin with: the common good. Ultimately, the common good we all share and desire is eternal beatitude with our Lord in heaven. And while the state cannot bring about our salvation, it *can* produce conditions favorable for the salvation of souls.

A good society makes it as easy as possible for people—all people, not just the rich and respectable—to follow God's will. Most of the time, this means the everyday task of growing in virtue and holiness. But when God's will is unveiled to us in a special and sometimes frightening way, we need to be ready and able to change course.

This means that a good society will focus on providing broadly-shared economic and social stability so that little apocalypses can be met with confidence in the Lord's providence rather than despair in our powerlessness. We often forget (or ignore) the list of rights and duties the Church has taught are essential to order and justice:

Man has the right to live. He has the right to bodily integrity and to the means necessary for the proper development of life, particularly food, clothing, shelter, medical care, rest, and, finally, the necessary social services. In consequence, he has the right to be looked after in the event of ill health; disability stemming from his work; widowhood; old age; enforced unemployment; or whenever through no fault of his own he is deprived of the means of livelihood.[2]

If this list seems extravagant, even radical, this is only because we have lived for too long in a society that denies these essentials to too many of our fellow men. The means of the provision of these rights is, of course, debatable, but their necessity is not.

*   *   *

The Church has a special role to play in creating and maintaining a society open to *apokalypsis*. This is most obviously true in the supernatural order—the order of grace. Participation in the sacramental life of the Church is absolutely essential to developing a confident openness to God's will. Further, the supernatural common good—eternal beatitude—is the exclusive purview of the Church. This is the theme of much of the rest of this book.

---

[2] Pope John XXIII, Encyclical Letter on Establishing Universal Peace in Truth, Justice, Charity, and Liberty *Pacem in Terris* (April 11, 1963), §11.

But the Church is also by necessity active in the order of nature. Attempts to sequester the Church to the supernatural realm are intellectually misguided, socially damaging, and doomed to failure. Jesus Christ is King of Heaven *and* Earth; the Church, as His bride and the conveyor of His grace, is necessarily and uniquely a part of both the supernatural and natural orders.

Therefore, in addition to preparing the faithful for the little apocalypses of life spiritually, parishes and apostolates and ministries prepare them in more prosaic ways, such as social and financial support. Local parishes are and must be more than one-hour-per-week worship sites. When the faith is reduced to a once-a-week obligation, it merely confirms the prevailing notion that "religion" is just one aspect of life among many—one that we should put aside in order to participate in the everyday secular world.

Liturgy is central to the Church's mission in both the order of nature and the order of grace; the Mass is in a real sense heaven on earth. If a parish does nothing else besides the Mass, it still provides a service of incalculable value to the community. Nothing can replace the Eucharist. But that doesn't mean we should rest; priests and lay people can participate in the work of God in many other ways in their communities.

By being active in as many areas of life as possible, the Church reflects the truth that faith cannot be pigeonholed as a "merely religious" concern. The parish should, as far as possible, be the center of all life for the faithful. In so doing, it becomes a living rebuke to a hostile culture while serving parishioners and the wider community the fruits of heaven and of earth.

The key concept is *integration*. An integral Catholic community models the comprehensive integrity of the faith by admitting no separation between its spiritual services and its social services. We should neither accept being sequestered to the "religious sphere" of life nor try to act like a secular nonprofit; both courses acquiesce to an unacceptable status quo. In forming integral communities, we become prophetic signs of contradiction, and we model the kind of community that should, well, *integrate* all humanity.

* * *

Following God's will for us isn't always practical, as that word is widely understood. It may not impress your boss to arrive late or leave early from work to attend Mass on a holy day of obligation. It may hurt your finances to turn down a job opportunity that would require unacceptable compromises of morality or family duties. It may seem extravagant for a church to spend money on precious metals and beautiful art.

But these actions are only "impractical" if we restrict ourselves to worldly concerns. And what could be more impractical than that? If "practicality" means the application of wisdom and prudence to particular circumstances, then it would be impractical in the extreme to simply ignore the most important participant in every moment of our lives: the Lord God.

By embracing a different and fuller practicality, the lives of Catholics in today's world will, like the Church herself, become signs of contradiction. And that is as it should be. We shouldn't fit comfortably into a culture that prizes only autonomy and writes God out of every story. We should feel out of place and, sometimes, we should look out of place.

We might go so far as to say that we should be people of the apocalypse—living in constant expectation of the little apocalypses of God's will for us, the regular apocalypse of the Mass, and the final apocalypse of His glory. That means living lives oriented first toward heaven and only secondly toward the world.

CHAPTER 10

The Personal Battle

P ersonal sanctity is a prerequisite for the success of all the social and political concepts I've covered in this book. No grand theories or perfect procedures can make up for a people who have abandoned virtue.

Thus far, I have examined the way marriage gives structure, sustainability, and meaning to society. Families are both the fundamental building blocks of human societies and the conceptual key for understanding them. Marriage is the indispensable institution; the family is the first society.

Further, I have sketched a Catholic vision for society that places the common good—not liberty or security or prosperity or equality or any other good-but-insufficient concept—at the very center. A society that takes the common good seriously will therefore take marriage seriously and will organize itself so as to make forming lasting marriages and robust families as easy as possible for us sinful creatures.

I have focused throughout this book on the communities and institutions—couples and families and governments and corporations—that make up the wider society as an implicit rebuke to an individualistic, secular liberalism. In a political culture where all sides in the mainstream discourse lavish attention on individual rights and liberties (even if they prioritize different ones), our privileging of communities, structures, and responsibilities is both an important corrective and a radical challenge. The Church's social vision does not and should not sit comfortably in liberal societies of the twenty-first century.

And yet we cannot ignore the individual altogether. While we are made *for* community just as the triune God is a community of love, we are made *as* individuals just as Jesus Christ is an individual man. Our dignity as persons created in God's image inheres in us as individuals, not as members of familial, ethnic, or national communities. And our relationship with the Lord is not mediated through any other person or human institution; it is truly personal.

No matter how "perfect" the organization of a society and government might be, it can't make us good. A well-ordered society would make it easier to be good, but it can't do the work of individual sanctification that is between each of us and the Lord. All of these grand ideas about communities, the state, and the common good will only bear fruit in a society full of individual people striving for holiness.

*   *   *

Here's the problem: we can't wait around for conditions to improve before going about the hard work of growing in virtue. A better world won't just appear, ready for us to slide comfortably in with a routine of prayer and habitual virtue. We have to get our own spiritual house in order amid the unpredictable whirlwind of a secular and alienated age before we can even begin to plan for a more godly future.

One of the most important concepts to keep in focus as we undertake this challenging task is *integrity*. In previous chapters I've used the converse, *disintegration*, to describe what happens to families and societies in thrall to individualism. A thing maintains its integrity by remaining whole—that is, by keeping united that which ought to be united. Dis-integration, then, is dividing that which ought to be whole, causing the whole to lose not just its oneness, but often its very identity. (When a sandcastle disintegrates, it doesn't just become a broken sandcastle; rather, it ceases to be a sandcastle altogether.)

Modern secular liberalism doesn't just disintegrate families and other communities; it encourages the disintegration of individual persons. Think of all the ways we are encouraged to artificially divide our lives: we (especially men) are supposed to embrace irresponsibility and promiscuity in our younger years, then magically settle down to monogamy once the vows are taken. We are supposed to compartmentalize work and family (and often other parts of life), enforcing a strict separation as if we can, for instance, suspend our family identities in the workplace. And we are supposed to keep our faith sequestered within the four walls of the church in order to maintain a properly secular public square.

In these ways and many more we are constantly challenged to maintain the integrity of our lives—the integrity we were made for and that God asks of us. All of these dis-integrations share the implication that there are parts of our lives when our duties, both to God and our fellow men, are suspended. Youthful sexual exploits are excused and even praised as "experimentation"; checking one's family identity at the entrance of the workplace is called "professionalism"; pretending God doesn't matter once Mass is over is required due to "respect" and "tolerance." No, no, and definitely no. It's one of the slyest tricks the devil tries to play—convincing us not that rules and duties have vanished, but that they simply don't apply at the moment.

We must pray constantly for integrity—for the grace to live our lives with unity and completeness, and to resist the temptations toward disintegration that are all around us. St. Paul wrote:

> Do you not know that in a race all the runners compete, but only one receives the prize? So run that you may obtain it. Every athlete exercises self-control in all things. They do it to receive a perishable wreath, but we an imperishable. Well, I do not run aimlessly, I do not box as one beating the air; but I pommel my body and subdue it, lest after preaching to others I myself should be disqualified. (1 Cor 9:24–27)

The race is never suspended; if we are not advancing, then we are losing ground. While every stage and state in life comes with its own duties and priorities, the integrity of the human person demands that we never let our *first* identity in Christ and our *first* duties to the Lord fade into the background.

*   *   *

Lust may be the most personally and socially disintegrating of the vices. Lust separates us from others by setting up a subject-to-object relationship between us and the targets of our gazes. This in turn separates us from our very selves, as the objectification of other persons infects the way we think about our own humanity.

The Catechism of the Catholic Church identifies the disintegrating nature of lust right in its definition: "Lust is disordered desire for or inordinate enjoyment of sexual pleasure. Sexual pleasure is morally disordered when sought for itself, *isolated from its procreative and unitive purposes*" (CCC 2351; emphasis added). Lust removes the other-regarding aspects of sexuality—"its procreative and unitive purposes"—leaving only the self-regarding pursuit of pleasure and power.

Lust also effects a disintegration of the person into "body" and "soul." Other people become, to our eyes, simply bodies designed for our personal enjoyment rather than integrated persons—embodied souls. We soon see ourselves as flesh detached from the soul—flesh from which we can derive pleasure at our will's command. We objectify our very selves, annihilating our true nature as integrated creatures made in God's image.

This is naturally deeply corrosive to the integrity of the marital relationship, which requires spouses to give themselves to one another completely—body and soul integrated. Under the dominion of lust, even marital sexual intercourse becomes a kind of virtual reality as bodies flop around pleasurably while spouses fail to be truly and fully *present* to each other. This is the carnal equivalent of nodding while your spouse talks when you're actually listening to loud music.

The latter might be communication, strictly speaking, and the former might be sex, strictly speaking, but both lack the proper end of those actions: communion.

*   *   *

It would be easy to blame our coarse and crass culture for the particularly strong temptation of lust, but the Catechism wisely recognizes the timelessness of discord emerging from sexual disorder:

> Every man experiences evil around him and within himself. This experience makes itself felt in the relationships between man and woman. Their union has always been threatened by discord, a spirit of domination, infidelity, jealousy, and conflicts that can escalate into hatred and separation. This disorder can manifest itself more or less acutely, and can be more or less overcome according to the circumstances of cultures, eras, and individuals, *but it does seem to have a universal character.* (CCC 1606; emphasis added)

This passage lists several vices that threaten marriage, but all of them have their root in the disintegration and objectification that are inherent in lust. Like all sins, lust pretends to reveal and fulfill our deepest desires when in fact it obscures our view of the truth, of Christ, of others, and of our true selves.

While advertising, popular culture, and especially pornography have laid out conditions under which lust can flourish, disordered desires have marred the male–female relationship since the Fall. While building a culture less favorable to the capital sin of lust must be a priority, we cannot scapegoat "the culture" for our own struggles. It's our job to fight lust in our hearts.

*   *   *

These three sentences from St. Josemaría Escrivá, the great twentieth-century saint and founder of Opus Dei, give us the fundamental order of battle for spiritual warfare:

> Anyone who wants to fight [spiritual battle] has to use the available means, which have not changed in twenty centuries of Christianity. They are prayer, mortification, and frequent use of the sacraments. Since mortification is also prayer—prayer of the senses—we can sum up these means in two words: prayer and sacraments.[1]

Lust may sometimes feel uncontrollable, but with prayer, mortification, and sacraments, we have all the resources we need to rein it in and defeat it. Remember always what the Lord told St. Paul: "My grace is sufficient for you, for my power is made perfect in weakness" (2 Cor 12:9).

Let's begin with prayer and mortification. What does St. Josemaría mean when he says that mortification is "prayer of the senses"? In the same way that prayer lifts our souls

---

[1] Josemaría Escrivá de Balaguer, *Christ Is Passing By* (New York: Scepter, 2002), no. 78.

to God, mortification—that is, habits of self-denial such as fasting and abstinence—lift our bodies to God. Therefore, mortification is simply a subset of prayer, but one that is essential to the integral nature of man—body and soul.

St. Josemaría writes: "Mortification is the seasoning of our life. And the best mortification is that which overcomes the lust of the flesh, the lust of the eyes, and the pride of life in little things throughout the day."[2] In other words, the most effective mortifications are not always huge (and sometimes showy) impositions we place on ourselves, but little (and sometimes unnoticeable) decisions that put others first: selecting the least desirable piece of pizza, cheerfully watching your spouse's favorite TV program, and so on. These little mortifications acclimate us to thinking of our duties to others and the Lord so that when, for instance, lust attacks us in earnest, we are ready.

In the same way, prayer need not mean immediate commitments to full-family rosaries or hours of adoration—though those things are very good and should be among our spiritual goals. Forming habits of prayer begins with little evocations of God throughout the day: a fifteen-second morning offering, a five-second prayer of thanksgiving for having been delivered to work safely, a silent petition for a family member who seems troubled. In this way we become, like with mortification, accustomed to appealing to the Lord when trouble finds us.

Prayer of the mind and body heals the disintegration caused by sins such as lust by reintegrating us with the perfect life and love of Jesus Christ, and thus with those

---

[2] Ibid., no. 9.

around us and with ourselves. That doesn't mean it happens easily or automatically. Prayer isn't magic. It is a constant struggle—a war—to identify and heal the wounds caused by sin. But we aren't in this alone—indeed, we can't go it alone. We always have recourse to the Church Triumphant—the Communion of Saints—in our prayers,[3] but here I'd like to focus on liturgy and the sacraments.

* * *

St. Josemaría pulls no punches: "If the sacraments are abandoned, genuine Christian life disappears."[4] He means this both personally and communally. Regular reception of the sacraments is an integral part of being a Christian and is essential to any plan of spiritual battle:

> But fighting calls for training, a proper diet, urgent medical attention in the case of illness, bruises and wounds. The sacraments are the main medicine the Church has to offer. They are not luxuries. If you voluntarily abandon them, it is impossible to advance on the road, to follow Jesus Christ. We need them as we need air to breathe, the circulation of the blood, and light to appreciate at every moment what our Lord wants of us.[5]

Whereas in prayer we lift ourselves up to God, in the sacraments He comes down to us. The Sacrament of Confession,

---

[3] See Hahn, *Angels and Saints*.
[4] Escrivá, *Christ Is Passing By*, no. 78.
[5] Ibid., no. 80.

which St. Josemaría calls the "tribunal of divine justice and especially of mercy,"[6] accentuates Jesus' spiritual nature and the Eucharist accentuates His physicality. Taken together, these regularly available sacraments remind us of the integral physical and spiritual nature we share with Jesus Christ.

Liturgy and the sacraments also bring us together in order to share our struggles and to share in God's grace. Even in the privacy of the confessional with a priest acting *in persona Christi* we are still entering a kind of communion both with the Lord and with another person. And, of course, in the Mass the congregation prays and receives the Eucharist together. The Communion of the Eucharist is with Jesus Christ, not the congregation, but there still is a different and lesser kind of small-"c" communion as we approach Him together.

Individual prayer and communal liturgy together reflect the unity-in-trinity of God in whose image human beings are created. The universality of the faith—its catholicity—is so often marked not by *either/or* but *both/and*: both individual and communal, both soul and body, both spiritual and physical. We represent and experience these integral truths by embracing them in our prayer and worship.

*   *   *

The solution to lust is in one sense extremely simple: the grace of God. Asking for and cooperating with that grace is the hard part, and there's no special cocktail of prayers and mortifications and liturgies that will magically perfect

---

6   Ibid., no. 78.

our souls; God is not bound by our mechanistic ways of thinking. And yet even in periods of spiritual dryness we are confident that grace abounds in the sacraments.

We are called to live sacramentally. Just as the sacraments are the center of the life of the Church, they should be at the center of the life of individuals, families, and communities. They should be just as much a part of daily life as eating breakfast and getting the mail. We should speak about them with the same familiarity and ease with which we discuss sports or the weather. The sacraments should not occupy an obscure corner of our lives dedicated to "religious things"; rather, they should be central to our lives because they are life-giving.

In discussions of the importance of the sacraments in spiritual battle we always mention Confession and the Eucharist because we receive them regularly. But marriage is just as much an outpouring of grace as any other sacrament; it may entail a one-time ceremony, but the grace associated with it lasts a lifetime.

Therefore, any commitment to living sacramentally must, as an individual, as a family, or as a society, include marriage not just as a sociological phenomenon, but as a sacrament.

CHAPTER 11

Redeeming Marriage through Sacrament

"The sanctity of marriage" has become a popular political buzz phrase, used by some to defend traditional marriage laws and by others to mock the idea that marriage has any sanctity left. I sympathize with both sides in this political mud fight.

On the one hand, marriage, considered sacramentally or just naturally, is truly a sacred institution. It was established by God and images the Trinity. The ultimate blessing of new life—new souls minted by God Himself and ordered toward eternal communion with Him—emerges from the marriage bond. Yes, marriage has sanctity.

And yet who could deny that the "traditional marriage" of twenty-first-century America has become a farce? Long before the words "same-sex marriage" entered the public lexicon, no-fault divorce swept the country and marriage breakup rates soared to 50 percent. And before that, all laws restricting artificial contraception had been swept away; consequently, the prevailing assumption for at least two generations has been that there is no inherent connection between marriage and procreation. They're two totally distinct choices a couple might make. Yes, the practice of marriage in America and around the Western world has ignored and undermined its sanctity.

The entire controversy over same-sex "marriage" is merely a consequence of our inability to live within even the most basic parameters of natural marriage. The LGBT movement didn't destroy marriage; any culture with a decent respect for marriage would find the concept of same-sex "marriage" utterly incomprehensible. That is: any society in which the idea of same-sex "marriage" can gain a foothold has already lost its marriage culture.

Once we've lost the meaning and purpose of marriage, anything can go. Plural marriage is gaining steam as polyamorous groups—that is, groups of more than two people who live together and have sexual relationships with one another—increase in number and visibility. The concept of the "wed lease"—a temporary but renewable marriage contract—has been floated in prominent publications. The venerable Oxford University Press recently published a collection of essays entitled *After Marriage* in which academics suggested ways to radically reshape the institution, from decriminalizing polygamy and separating parenting from marriage to abolishing marriage altogether. Even *Good Housekeeping*, the venerable mainstream women's magazine known mostly for casserole recipes and Crock-Pot reviews, recently reported approvingly on a new marriage trend: self-marriages.

This is all quite troubling, to be sure. But we can't allow ourselves to be satisfied pointing the finger at polyamorous quintets and self-wedding narcissists and saying, "Aha! They are the problem with marriage!" We would do better to remember the famous declaration popularized in the *Pogo* comic strip back in the 1970s, right as marriage was being gutted from within and without: "We have met the enemy, and he is us." This didn't happen overnight; it didn't even only start in the 1960s. There will be no rebuilding of a culture of marriage until we, as Christians and specifically as Catholics, begin to live out the truth of marriage as God intended it.

*   *   *

We are experiencing a feedback loop: new ideas and technologies undermined the historic understanding of marriage as both a natural and a sacramental institution. No longer understanding what marriage is and can be, our living-out of marriage declined both in the raw number of marriages and in the quality of marriages that were actually formed. Our poor execution of the duties of marriage then further corroded our understanding of its true nature. Which, in turn, has led to a further degradation in the living-out of marriage . . .

How do we stop this process? Is there some magic pixie dust we can toss on this descending feedback loop that will not only arrest it but restore the original state of things?

It is a distinctively American assumption that with the right amount of elbow grease and duct tape we can fix anything. And so we look at marriage and say: "If only we could, through the hard work of persuasion, rediscover and spread among the people the historic understanding of marriage, then we can stop and reverse current trends!"

This is the wrong approach for two reasons. First, remember that one of the main premises of this book is that this is no time for nostalgia or rose-colored glasses. The language of "reversal" and "restoration" assumes that there is some satisfactory recent past to which we can and should return. But it's a mirage. We must be forward-looking, trying to build a future with the best lessons from the past rather than recreating the past.

Second, the focus on persuasion introduces a limitation to the proposed solution. But participation in the battlefield of persuasion requires playing by the secular rules of the modern public square—what the late Fr. Richard John Neuhaus called, all the way back in 1984, the "naked public square." Appeals to faith and grace and Scripture and revelation are forbidden. Therefore, the only marriage we are allowed to argue for in the public sphere is natural marriage—not sacramental marriage.

We may argue for all the marks of natural marriage—permanence and exclusivity and openness to life—which are accessible to natural reason, but we may not speak of the divine grace of the Sacrament of Matrimony. The best we could hope for, then, is a reemergence of the public understanding of *natural* marriage. And while that would be an improvement over the status quo, it would not be nearly enough.

As I argued back in chapter four, marriage at the individual level is impossible without the grace of the sacrament. How much more impossible, then, must a culture of marriage be without a public understanding of and appreciation for the sacramentality of marriage?

There is, I should mention, an opportunity for ecumenical cooperation here. To the extent certain Protestant denominations recognize the true nature of marriage, they too participate in the sacrament and can therefore participate in the reinvigoration of the public understanding of that sacramentality.

*   *   *

Intact things are easier to handle than broken ones. Imagine a grocery bag that tears, or a fold-up tent before and after all the pieces have been snapped together: intact, they can be held and carried and placed; broken, there are too many falling and flopping pieces for two arms to handle.

It is the same with natural marriage and sinful men and women. If we were perfect, the duties and challenges of marriage would pose no problem for us. All we would need is the proper understanding of what marriage is and we could live it out without a second thought—like robots obeying their software.

But we are broken, messy sinners—every last one of us. Maintaining natural marriage as the social ideal could sustain a society of perfect people, but it cannot bear the complicated weight of brokenness. We are not androids who execute God's will with precision and without hesitation; we rebel every day just as our first parents rebelled in the garden.

If we only aim for a society built just around natural marriage, denuded of divinity and sacramentality, we might achieve it—but not for long. Even if we all had a perfect (secular) understanding of permanence and exclusivity and openness to life—and even if divorce and artificial contraception were banned by law—we would find the expectations of marriage impossible and intolerable.

Without the healing power of God's grace, our brokenness would immediately reassert itself, each person's in its own unique way. The resulting new feedback loop would gut the renascent culture of marriage: the living out of marriage would degrade as people cut corners and ignored strictures, which would in turn degrade the norms we fought so hard to establish. Remember that marriage without God is possible in theory, but not in practice.

The promotion of a secularized vision of natural marriage is often a good-faith attempt to make the truth of marriage accessible and acceptable to a secular liberal society. The unfortunate irony is that it is precisely that which makes it acceptable—its removal of anything supernatural—that makes it unsustainable. Stripped-down natural marriage might be an easier sell at first, but only sacramental marriage can form a solid foundation for social order.

We remember, of course, the admonition in Hebrews: "For here we have *no lasting city*, but we seek the city which is to come" (Heb 13:14; emphasis added). Every political and social order disintegrates under the corrosive influence of sin, which can never be fully uprooted from our nature on this side of the veil; there is no perfectly sustainable order. But this is not a license to despair—to throw up our hands and say "anything goes" because it will all fall apart no matter what. Our duty is to provide for the common good in a sustainable way as well as we possibly can; secularized natural marriage is not a suitable foundation for such an effort.

*   *   *

But there's another problem with advocating for marriage without acknowledging its sacramental nature: it gets marriage wrong. Remember from back in chapter four: sacramentality isn't a bonus feature that we layer on top of natural marriage; rather, it's essential to *what marriage is* under the New Covenant. Arguing for a public understanding of marriage that subtracts its sacramental nature is like giving a speech in which one replaces all instances of the word "the" with the word "baseball." It doesn't make sense. What this means is that, as Catholics, we can't play ball with secularists with regard to the language of marriage.

Just because the powers-that-be in our country have no idea what "sacramentality" is and couldn't tell the New Covenant from the New Deal doesn't mean that they are not subject to the truths of sacramentality and the New Covenant. The potential of entering into a family relationship with God—the fundamental promise of the New Covenant—extends to our secular elite just as much as it does to you and me.

Marriage is intrinsically covenantal not just for Catholics but for everyone, whether they recognize it or not.[1] We can fail to recognize its covenantal nature, but our subjective misunderstanding of marriage doesn't change the objective reality. Civil marriage, therefore, is an incomplete attempt to mimic sacramental marriage.

The Church's truth is not suspended in a secular culture, nor is our duty to express it in its fullness. But we do not only

---

[1] See Gordon P. Hugenberger, *Marriage as a Covenant: Biblical Law and Ethics as Developed from Malachi* (Ada, MI: Baker Academic, 1998).

obscure the true nature of marriage when we neuter its sacramentality; we also obscure the true nature of the common good. The fact is that society *needs sacramental marriages.* The structure and sustainability of society depends not just on a commitment to the marital responsibilities that we can deduce from nature, but on the grace of God that flows through the Sacrament of Matrimony.

*   *   *

Let's pause for a quick review of the relationship between the Church, God's grace, and the sacraments. Jesus Christ established the Catholic Church, and it is His spouse. From that moment until the end of time, the Church is charged with keeping the sacraments—sacraments that were themselves established by Jesus. The sacraments, as covenant oaths,[2] confirm and renew the covenantal relationship between God and His people.

As such, the sacraments are not *just* symbols or rituals; they are symbols and rituals that actually convey the grace of God to His people. This is not a metaphor or abstraction; in the proper performance of a sacrament of the Church, we can say with certainty that the subject or subjects of the sacrament receive the gift of God's grace. The Church, therefore, is the medium through which grace is bestowed on humanity.

Our salvation depends on this grace, and so our salvation depends on the Church. All growth in holiness that

---

[2] See Scott Hahn, *Swear to God: The Promise and Power of the Sacraments* (New York: Image, 2004).

we experience has the grace of God as its ultimate cause. Everything good in this world comes from Him. We cannot be the people God made us to be without the Church and the sacraments over which she serves as custodian. Everything in the preceding three paragraphs is basic Church teaching, from the Church Fathers through today. It finds its source in the Word of God. It has survived heresies and challenges of all sorts. Everyone agrees that believing these truths is essential to the Catholic faith.

But that agreement dissolves when the obvious corollary is stated: the Church is essential to society—not just as a bit player or one option among many, but as the most indispensable institution in society. But how could it be otherwise? The necessity of God's grace doesn't fade when we pull the camera back from the individual to bring the community into view, and therefore neither does the necessity of the Church.

In later chapters I will go further, explaining how the Church is more than just the *central institution* in society: she already *is* a society—the heavenly society to which we must conform ourselves. But for now let us just say this: if we're serious about creating a vital and sustainable culture of marriage (and therefore a vital and sustainable society), we must be honest about the central role of God and His Church in that culture. God's grace is oxygen for the flame of marriage; our secular, liberal civilization smothers it.

*   *   *

Make no mistake about it: this is a radical claim in today's world. We have grown accustomed to a political system that claims to privilege no religion or ideology while enshrining secular liberalism as the lodestar of acceptability. We're used to critiquing the second part of that state of affairs—the raising of secular liberalism to the status of an established religion—but what about the first? Should our government and society privilege no religion above another?

If what I've said so far about marriage and sacraments and grace is true, then it would seem that it can be no better for the *community* to be indifferent to religious truth than for the *individual* to be indifferent to religious truth. In the same way that Jesus Christ and His bride the Church must be at the very center of our hearts, so must they also be at the very center of society. The common good, both in terms of our earthly duties and our heavenly destination, demands it.

This claim doesn't just implicate our modern secular elite; it also calls the wisdom of the American Founders into question. Partisans can argue forever about whether "the Founders" were more Enlightenment atheists or devout Christians—the truth is certainly somewhere in between— but everybody knows they weren't intending to give the Catholic Church pride of place in their new country. In fact, the Church's claims to be *the* bearer of truth and *the* custodian of the sacraments were considered threatening to their political project *precisely because* those claims imply a central role for the Church in civil affairs.

For this reason, anti-Catholic sentiment has a long history in American society, finally falling more or less out of favor with the 1960 election of John F. Kennedy. While that prejudice was often exacerbated by fever-dream hob-goblins in the Protestant imagination that bore no relation whatsoever to actual Catholicism, let's not be coy: there was an element of truth. The role the Church has claimed and should continue to claim for herself is in serious tension with the Protestant/Enlightenment ideals of America's founding and subsequent history.

Here is a representative anti-Catholic political cartoon with a sensational caption from the early twentieth century:

Romanism is a Monster, with arms of Satanic power and strength, reaching to the very ends of the earth, the arm of superstition crushing the American child, that of subversion crushing the American Flag, that of bigotry crushing the American Public School, that of ignorance crushing the law of the land, that of greed grasping public moneys, that of tyranny destroying freedom of conscience, freedom of speech, freedom of the press, all over the world—per totam orbem terrarum.

While much of that caption is insane, let's focus for a moment on "subversion." In the cartoon it's the most front-and-center tentacle of the octopus, and it's grasping an American flag while breaking its staff in two. The implication is that Catholics have a temporal allegiance higher than their allegiance to the United States—an allegiance to the Church. Well, we do! This doesn't mean we can't also love and respect our country—indeed we should do so as far as we are able to. But we must remember that we are always, by virtue of our faith in Jesus Christ, "strangers in a strange land," as Archbishop Charles Chaput of Philadelphia puts it in the title of his book.[3]

If it's unacceptable for Catholics to hold our Church closer than our nation, that's a problem with our society, not with our faith. And if it's unthinkable for the Church to have pride of place in civil society, that's a problem with our nation's understanding of itself, not with the Church's understanding of herself.

*   *   *

Back in chapter nine, I said that taking God's will seriously requires a "fuller practicality"—one that takes into account both supernatural truths and worldly concerns. Again, what is the case for individuals is also the case for communities. A practical politics isn't one that ignores God; to the contrary, taking politics seriously requires taking God, His Church, and His grace seriously.

It's a popular progressive conceit that if we only had more information—more data, more studies, more "science"—we could have a more rational politics. But the data our politics is missing doesn't necessarily come from the order of nature, but from the order of grace. A society that recognizes the

---

[3]   See Charles Chaput, *Strangers in a Strange Land: Living the Catholic Faith in a Post-Christian World* (New York: Henry Holt, 2017).

truth of human dignity and the common good is impossible without integrating the order of grace into politics.

But how does this grace I keep talking about work? How does grace help us become holy, and how does it allow us to build a more perfect society? Let's explore how grace perfects nature.

CHAPTER 12

Grace Perfects Nature

A young friend recently told me about an experience he and his wife had at Mass. Their two toddlers were visiting with family and so they were able to go to church by themselves for a change.

It was the kind of reverent liturgy that makes you wish all Masses could be celebrated with such solemnity. After Holy Communion, as the couple knelt to pray, my friend heard his wife quietly sobbing. Knowing that she had been physically and emotionally overwhelmed by their rambunctious toddlers and her third pregnancy, he asked what was wrong. But her response was not at all what he expected: she had experienced an overpowering sensation of peace—what could only be described as the grace of God—as she accepted and consumed the Body of Christ.

The reality of grace, of course, doesn't depend on having an intense experience like this one. Most sacraments feel perfectly mundane even as they are, in fact, incredibly powerful spiritual gifts. What examples like this give us, though, is the tiniest taste of what it will *feel* like to share completely in God's life in heaven. If one fleeting moment here on earth can create a lifelong memory, imagine how beautiful it will be to experience that divine life and love in its fullness for eternity.

Let's dig a little deeper into what grace is and how it functions in the lives of God's adopted children.

*   *   *

Grace is impossible to describe completely; anything totally of God cannot be fully explained with the limitations imposed by human language. The moment we try to put anything about God's life and nature into words, we have limited Him who is limitless.

And that is what grace is: "participation in the life of God." The sections of the Catechism of the Catholic Church about grace, to which I will refer throughout this chapter, are especially beautiful. Grace "introduces us into the intimacy of Trinitarian life. . . . As an 'adopted son' [the baptized] can henceforth call God 'Father,' in union with the only Son. He receives the life of the Spirit who breathes charity into him and who forms the Church" (CCC 1997). Grace makes us family.

St. Thomas Aquinas taught that we can only approach understanding the nature of God by analogy. God is too big, too loving, too perfect, too *everything* for our measly brains to comprehend. And so our discussion of grace in this chapter will be based on human actions and categories that will allow us to think about God by reference to familiar concepts. But we must always remember: we can only ever scratch the surface of understanding what grace is and how it functions in our lives (CCC 40–43).

(But here's the beautiful thing: through grace we can reach understandings beyond anything we can dream. That is what heaven is—a complete sharing of God's life, including His knowledge. And sometimes, in what are called "actual graces," God intervenes in our lives and reveals truths to us in a special way [CCC 2000].)

The ways grace functions in our lives can't be numbered. Indeed, we owe our lives themselves—the consciousness by which we can read books like this and raise our hearts to heaven and contemplate the divine—to God's grace. But we can use three particular actions to describe how grace works that will help us to understand it a little bit better: grace heals; grace perfects; grace elevates.

*   *   *

Grace heals the effects of sin. Sin wounds the soul like an injury wounds the body. The truly perverse thing about sin is that we *choose* it; we inflict the injury on our own souls in pursuit of some perceived greater good—usually pleasure or power or some other sensation. But the grace of Christ is "infused by the Holy Spirit into our soul to heal it of sin and to sanctify it" (CCC 1999).

Our bodies heal themselves, though sometimes we can help things along. This is how healing works in the order of nature: our bodies tend to themselves and we tend to each other. This doesn't mean there is no spiritual element to physical healing; as integrated spiritual and physical beings, we can never fully separate the two—and God can work miracles in either the physical or spiritual realms as He pleases.

And yet there is a necessary distinction between healing of the body and healing of the soul. Whereas, since we exist in time and space, we take the lead in physical healing (though, again, nothing is beyond God's purview), spiritual healing can only be accomplished by God. We can *participate* in this healing by *cooperating* with His grace, but we cannot bandage sin like a paper cut.

The most obvious locus of this healing grace is in the sacraments, beginning with Baptism. Since the Fall, every person (other than the Blessed Mother) has shared in the first sin of pride and disobedience committed by Adam and Eve; this is what we call original sin. How beautiful it is that in every one of the baptisms that have been performed over the last two thousand years, God has healed that inherited wound. He has, through the grace of the sacrament, not just forgiven but erased the deeply personal betrayal of His first human creations more than a billion times over.

Sin disorients us; that is, it knocks us off-kilter from our proper orientation toward God. Our errors then compound themselves, each one making rediscovering the proper path increasingly difficult. Baptism, however, starts us out on the straight and narrow. Then, once we have developed the ability to choose willfully against the good, we promptly do so, losing our orientation. God's grace—especially in the Sacraments of the Eucharist and Confession—constantly puts us back on track. Grace heals not just the spiritual wound but the resulting confusion that muddles our reasoning and our contemplation.

But these actions of grace always require our cooperation. God does not compel; after all, our free will is part of our participation in His nature, in the *imago Dei*: "God's free initiative demands *man's free response*, for God has created man in his image by conferring on him, along with freedom, the power to know him and love him" (CCC 2002; emphasis added). It is up to us to approach the Eucharist with our soul in order; it is up to us to enter the confessional with a spirit of true contrition; it is up to us to accept the Lord's invitation back to Him.

*   *   *

Grace perfects human nature. The healing effected by the grace of Christ makes it possible for us to become the people—the beings—God made us to be. He did not make us for pride and greed and lust; but for perfection, and true perfection can only be found in Him. He made us for Himself not in the sense of ownership, but in the sense of familial love—a spirit of adoption that is made possible by the gift of His life that is grace.

But part of being made in God's image is free will; we are given the *possibility* but not the *assurance* of perfection. This isn't some kind of perverse sadism as God gleefully watches us flail about helplessly. Just the opposite: our free will makes us His most beloved creatures because our acceptance of Him is freely chosen and ongoing. Further, the weakness of our will demonstrates the perfection of His strength as He heals and perfects our disobedient will.

The purification of our will—that is, the conforming of our will to the Lord's—is therefore a partnership. How beautiful it is that the all-powerful Lord condescends to become our copilot as we try to navigate our lives toward Him! Our effort and His grace work together; both aspects are essential. But God is always the first mover:

> The *preparation of man* for the reception of grace is already a work of grace. . . . God brings to completion in us what he has begun, "since he who completes his work by cooperating with our will began by working so that we might will it" [St. Augustine, *De gratia et libero arbitrio*, 17:PL 44,901]. (CCC 2001)

In other words, God not only brings us to perfection; He also initiates the desire for that perfection.

The perfection of our nature is not found in becoming fully our own, but in conforming our will to the Lord's. This task is only achievable with the gratuitous help of God that we call grace.

*   *   *

Grace elevates us so that we become "partakers of the divine nature" (2 Pet 1:4). God's favor doesn't just allow us to become the best human beings we can be; it raises us to His level. We can go so far as to say that grace *deifies* us: "The grace of Christ is the gratuitous gift that God makes to us of his own life. . . . It is . . . *sanctifying* or *deifying grace*" (CCC 1999; emphasis added). Grace, incredibly, allows us to become like God.

Let's focus for a moment on the word "gratuitous." We can never merit the elevation to godliness that grace accomplishes in us; that is, there is no collection of actions we can perform or doctrines we can believe that will *earn* our participation in the divine nature. Virtue and right belief are essential to accepting and cooperating with grace, but grace is always a gift and never compensation for services rendered. God is on such a different plane of power and perfection from us that we can never do anything to *earn* His favor.

And yet God can raise us to that plane of perfection, as the Catechism tells us:

> [Grace] brings about filial adoption so that men become Christ's brethren, as Jesus himself called his disciples after his Resurrection: "Go and tell my brethren" [Mt 28:10; Jn 20:17]. We are brethren not by nature, but by the gift of grace, because that adoptive filiation gains us a real share in the life of the only Son, which was fully revealed in his Resurrection. (CCC 654)

Grace makes possible what is impossible by our own efforts. We cannot cross the metaphysical chasm between us and God on our own, but He can bring us over to Him.

Let's now turn to how these actions of grace—healing, perfecting, elevating—work in our lives as individuals, families, and communities.

*　　*　　*

I have argued throughout this book that the responsibilities of marriage are impossible to fulfill without the grace of the

Sacrament of Matrimony. But how does that grace actually work? Grace, as we will see, makes the intense and unparalleled intimacy of marriage possible, enduring, and fruitful.

We often associate the word "intimate" only with sexuality and nudity (think the "intimates" section in a department store). This association brings out some important connotations—vulnerability and passion come to mind—but physical intimacy is only part of the story. The "one-flesh" union of husband and wife refers to more than just sex; it means spouses share their very minds and souls—their emotions, their intellects, their spiritualities—with one another.

But let's bring this down to earth: living together is hard. Habits and preferences clash; hidden tendencies and peccadillos are revealed; vices are magnified under the constant gaze of another person. I assiduously roll up the toothpaste tube; Kimberly does not. You can imagine the tension this causes.

This kind of complete communion of persons is part of the fulfillment of our nature as relational beings, but requires the kind of self-effacement and self-giving that our fallen wills rebel against violently. This is where the three actions of grace intervene on our behalf.

The healing power of grace restores to our souls the selflessness required to live the vocation of marriage. Sin, as I said earlier in this chapter, compounds itself. We become accustomed to it, and soon more and more of our lives become organized around our own (wrong) way of doing things rather than God's—and we often don't even realize it. This is exactly the kind of blind self-centeredness that slowly corrodes a marriage from the inside. Grace heals these effects of sin, opening our eyes both to the goodness of God's will and to the difficult truth of our own disordered desires.

The perfecting power of grace brings our will into accord not only with God's will, but with our relational nature. The Sacrament of Matrimony is not just a one-time outpouring of grace on the couple but a continual discharging of grace for as long as the parties to the marriage remain in God's friendship. If marital grace were a lottery jackpot, it would be an annuity rather than a lump sum. Here's the Catechism on this grace:

> This grace proper to the sacrament of Matrimony is intended to perfect the couple's love and to strengthen their indissoluble unity. . . .
>
> . . . Christ dwells with them, gives them the strength to take up their crosses and so follow him, to rise again after they have fallen, to forgive one another, to bear one another's burdens, to "be subject to one another out of reverence for Christ" [Eph 5:21; cf. Gal 6:2], and to love one another with supernatural, tender, and fruitful love. (1641–42)

Marriage fulfills our nature as relational beings, but God first needs to lay the foundation of desire for that fulfillment. Then He guides our will toward Him, drawing us out of ourselves and into communion with Him and other persons—especially those closest to us. In this way He not only makes us a more perfect version of ourselves, but He allows us to more perfectly image His relational, Trinitarian identity through marriage.

The elevating power of grace raises up our marriages to become living icons of the Most Holy Trinity. The triune God is both one and three—unity and community—and so we become most like Him when we enter into communion with others. We aren't just elevated to godliness as individuals; our marriages are elevated as perfect images of unity-in-community. The beautiful and brilliant miracle that grace effects in us is this: we become more fully our own *at the same time* that we give more of ourselves in this communion. We do this, of course, through self-giving love that both reflects and is initiated by the eternal love among the Father, the Son, and the Holy Spirit. This Trinitarian truth means that deification is *both* individual *and* communal.

*　　*　　*

On the other hand, sin breaks the bonds of community— the communion—we make with God and with one another and turns us inward to ourselves. Perhaps the most evocative image of this disintegration of bonds can be found in the Acts of the Apostles: as the eleven remaining apostles prayed over which disciple should take the place of Judas, they said that the betrayer "turned aside" from his apostleship "to go to his own place" (Acts 1:25). Sin isolates us; what could be lonelier than Judas' solitary suicide?

By healing our spiritual wounds, perfecting our nature, and elevating us to God's level, grace *makes community possible*. Under the dominion of sin we all go off to our own place—a place with our own morality, our own philosophy, our own truth. We are the king but, like the king of the vacant asteroid in Antoine de Saint-Exupéry's *The Little Prince*, we have no subjects. It is inexpressibly lonely.

Sin isolates; grace integrates. Only grace can sustain the communion that makes marriage possible. Therefore, only grace can sustain the communion—especially the abiding desire for the common good—that makes society possible. And therefore any enduring society must unite itself to the source of grace, Jesus Christ. *Totus Christus*—"Whole Christ"—would be a fitting aspirational motto for the Catholic social vision, in families, communities, and, God willing, entire societies. It is through the Church that we can achieve that total communion—with Christ, with the saints, and with each other.

CHAPTER 13

The Church's Unique Position

O ur secular liberal culture struggles to understand any-thing objective, enduring, and transcendent. For us, only subjective experiences make sense and only market-able commodities have value. But the Catholic faith is not a lifestyle choice, and the Church is not a consumer brand. What are good secular liberals to make of Catholicism?

Well, if we're being honest, they *should* find it at least a little bit frightening. The Catholic Church fails to play by their rules: she claims to be the bearer of truth when truth is considered passé. She claims to have temporal authority when religious institutions are supposed to stay in their "spiritual" lane. She claims to bestow value when the market is supposed to be the only arbiter of value. Finally, she claims all human beings have dignity when dignity is increasingly tied to usefulness. In doing these things, she provides the only substantial, comprehensive, and humane alternative to a secular and liberal regime that has sucked transcendence out of our civilization.

Unfortunately, we have spent the better part of the last century trying to assert what makes Catholics and Catholicism *acceptable* to secular liberals rather than accentuating our distinctiveness. Whether it takes the form of equivocation on hot-button issues like abortion and marriage or muting Catholic teaching on the rights of workers and immigrants, the trend has too often been to compromise our uniqueness in order to play ball with the powers-that-be. And in the end, of course, we just get co-opted, losing our Catholic identity and winning little influence.

In all of this, we end up treating ourselves just as secular liberalism wants to treat us—as one interest group among many jockeying for position on the greasy pole of coalition politics. We soon forget that the Church has anything unique to offer that isn't contingent on whether our political tribe has achieved fleeting power. We shunt liturgy and grace and the sacraments off to one side as merely religious concerns; we might offer a Mass for a political intention, but we can't see that the Mass by its very nature—heaven on earth!—has political implications. It's cultural and political Stockholm Syndrome: we have begun to identify with and act like our secular captors.

Remember what I said back in chapter seven: the word "catholic" is not a brand name for our church, but a descriptor of her universality. We can reckon the Church's universal nature in several ways. First, of course, the Body of Christ beckons all human beings to the divine embrace without prejudice or preference. But universality also means that the Church is not just "religious": her teaching and authority touch all aspects of the human experience—social, cultural, economic, political, and so on. It is precisely this catholicity that points to a way forward for a disintegrating civilization.

*   *   *

I could describe the horror of abortion in many ways. Most importantly, it is the intentional killing of an innocent human person. But it is a very particular type of killing—one that rends the social fabric in uniquely destructive ways. Abortion has been (quite profitably) institutionalized by billion-dollar concerns such as Planned Parenthood and is supported by legal regimes across the West—none more so than in the United States. And it strikes at the heart of solidarity, which is a central component of Catholic social teaching.

Institutionalized abortion severs the most fundamental locus of solidarity: the bond between parents and their children. The politically convenient rhetoric of "pro-choice" makes this even clearer than the more accurate "pro-abortion," since it reduces that essential parent–child duty to a choice. If even this responsibility—to nurture the helpless children in our care—is contingent on our will to carry it out, then what social duties could possibly have moral force?

If we, either as individual parents or as a society, have no duties to the unborn, on what ground can we have duties to workers or immigrants or oppressed minorities or the unemployed or the elderly or the disabled—all the people on the margins of society about whom the popes have spoken so forcefully? Abortion, then, is both a symptom and a cause of a solidarity-starved society.

SCOTT HAHN

I could say the same of no-fault divorce. Not only do all social bonds take their form from the universal hermeneutic of the family, but the family is the place where people first learn how to live out the reciprocal duties of solidarity. Taken together, institutionalized divorce and abortion sever the husband–wife and parent–child bonds, thereby removing the very foundation of solidarity on which social stability is built. There can be no solidarity when the reciprocal duties of family life are optional. How are young people to learn what it means to live in solidarity with their fellow human beings when there is no solidarity within their own families?

Should we be surprised, then, by the political and economic insecurity of this moment in history? Should we be surprised at the mistrust of all the institutions of our common life—legislatures and bureaucracies and corporations and so on? How should we be expected to trust distant authorities when so many cannot trust their own families or neighbors? And how should those authorities be expected to exercise power with magnanimity when we have gutted the traditional concept of social duties—especially duties to the weak and marginal?

We have seen such an incredible growth in prosperity and technological progress during the past few generations. And yet the social fabric is fraying. It seems that people—even those who have the means to purchase more than they could ever need—feel more uneasy and insecure than ever. And here's the darkest observation of all: under secularism, there are no solutions on the horizon.

*   *   *

Secularism cannot provide a basis for solidarity. Sure, secular liberals pay lip service to humanitarianism and the brotherhood of mankind, but drill down deeper into these secular platitudes and you find nothing but air. They cannot account for the uniqueness of human beings; they cannot account for the intrinsic value and dignity of every person; they cannot account for any kind of a purpose or *telos* (from the Greek for "end") to human existence.

And so secular liberals cannot account for solidarity except on the basis of the shared interest of autonomous individuals. This takes many forms, none of which are satisfactory. In what is often called "neoliberalism," it is said that global capitalism can bring all the people of the world together in the shared interest of prosperity. But this has entailed the imposition by the powerful on the powerless not only of dangerous jobs for paltry wages, but of "liberal values" such as abortion and sexual license—all in the name of building a "global marketplace." This is closer to colonialism than solidarity.

And this doesn't just take place *inter*-nationally, but also *intra*-nationally. In neighborhoods and entire regions across America, economic opportunity has dried up while "progressive" anti-family values have taken root. The question of which is more important to revitalization—economic opportunity or a culture of family—is a perennial and partisan chicken-and-egg problem, but let us just say this: the two clearly go hand in hand.

Faced with having been left out of the faux solidarity of neoliberalism, many are naturally looking elsewhere. And so we are seeing, across the Western world, a resurgence of the politics of ethnic and national identity. On the left, this often takes the form of the assertion of identity by groups that have been (or claim to have been) historically marginalized. On the right, this often takes the form of historically dominant groups reasserting their identitarian claims. In every case, identity politics is a counterfeit of true solidarity.

Secularism prohibits us from making the truly catholic claim that *all* believers are brothers and sisters in Christ and *all* human beings share in the *imago Dei*. Without the concept of an indivisible divinity in whose life we share through grace, we cannot comprehend, let alone live out, true solidarity.

*   *   *

And so what is true solidarity as the Church understands it? St. John Paul II defined the concept in this way in his 1987 encyclical *Sollicitudo Rei Socialis* ("The Social Concern"):

> It is above all a question of interdependence, sensed as a system determining relationships in the contemporary world, in its economic, cultural, political and religious elements, and accepted as a moral category. When interdependence becomes recognized in this way, the correlative response as a moral and social attitude, as a "virtue," is solidarity. This then is not a feeling of vague compassion or shallow distress at the misfortunes of so many people, both near and far. On the contrary, it is a firm and persevering determination to commit oneself to the common good; that is to say to the good of all and

of each individual, because we are all really responsible for all.[1]

Solidarity is the heart of the common good. A society that fails in solidarity also fails in the pursuit of the common good, which is its most basic function.

St. John Paul II goes on to identify two specific threats to solidarity and the development of healthy, integrated societies: the "desire for profit" and the "thirst for power." These selfish concerns are dis-integrative; they separate society between the powerful and the powerless, the useful and the useless. Written in 1987, these words were a rebuke of both the capitalism to the west of the Iron Curtain and the communism to the east of it.

Profit and power are two words for the same thing: the *libido dominandi*—a term coined by St. Augustine that means "the lust to dominate." It is the social manifestation of the original sin of Adam and Eve, the desire to be like God. The *libido dominandi* has been with us since the Fall and corrodes every interpersonal relationship, from marriage to the entire political community. How can we build a society under these conditions? St. John Paul II explains:

> These attitudes and "structures of sin" are only conquered—presupposing the help of divine grace—by a diametrically opposed attitude: a commitment to the good of one's neighbor with the readiness, in the gospel sense, to "lose oneself" for the sake of the

---

[1] Pope John Paul II, Encyclical Letter for the Twentieth Anniversary of *Populorum Progressio Sollicitudo Rei Socialis* (December 30, 1987), §38.

other instead of exploiting him, and to "serve him" instead of oppressing him for one's own advantage.[2]

Solidarity requires a radical commitment to the good of others over and above our own interests. But take note of that brief aside in John Paul's letter: "presupposing the help of divine grace."

Just as the grace of the Sacrament of Matrimony is essential to marriage, so is the grace of the Church essential to solidarity and, therefore, to a sustainable society that pursues the common good. The Catholic Church is the only answer to our present crisis.

*   *   *

The Western world has spent much of the last few centuries trying to find or form a replacement for the unifying catholicity of the Catholic Church. But the project has always been doomed to failure. No purely human idea or institution can replace the sacramental solidarity of the Church.

This is not to say that a society that rejects the authority of the Church can't exist, even for quite a long time. The United States was founded on an explicit denial of any particular religious authority over public affairs, and we've had a nearly two-hundred-fifty-year run—and counting! And yet the list of sins against solidarity we've committed in that time—including the American "original sin" of chattel slavery and a generally poor record with regard to racial and ethnic minorities, from indigenous Native Americans

---

[2]   Ibid.

to Chinese railroad workers—is long and damning. To be sure, every nation, like every person, has its sins; it's important, though, that we regard them with clear eyes. Every political order degrades under the influence of sin. As we read in Hebrews, "For here we have no lasting city, but we seek the city which is to come" (13:14). There is no perfect system. Even a political order founded and sustained by the Church cannot last forever; while the bride of Christ is indeed indwelt by the Holy Spirit, she is managed by sinful men. And yet we mustn't fall into despair and accept unacceptable compromises in the name of "political pragmatism." There is no "greater good"—whether prosperity or order or stability—that justifies acting against a precept of Jesus Christ and His Church. We never *have to* acquiesce in sin. And we do have a duty to our fellow men and women to create an order that is as stable and sustainable as flawed human beings can muster.

As the present age of secular liberalism grinds along falteringly, we are presented with a historic opportunity to rediscover and to reanimate the truth about Christ and society. The Church is more than just a salve for the alienation and ruination wrought by modern politics. She is even more than the central institution or organizing principle of a good society. Under the lordship of Jesus Christ and through the power of the Holy Spirit, constituted by the members of the Body of Christ on earth and in heaven, the Church is the perfect society.

Our duty, therefore, as the universal family of God, is to advance the liberty of the Catholic Church to fulfill its fully catholic mission in all areas of life.

*   *   *

It should feel strange—and maybe a bit scary—to read these words. They don't just challenge secularism; they challenge the classical foundations of liberal democracy and much of the postmodern West. But this shouldn't dissuade us from speaking up on behalf of this truth about Christ and the Church. In fact, it is precisely the radicalism of this claim that will make it appealing to more people than we think.

The questions we must ask ourselves are these: Do we really believe that human beings have a natural desire for truth, and that the Catholic Church and her Magisterium, under the guidance of the Holy Spirit, preserve the truth? And do we really believe that secular liberalism cannot fulfill the deepest longings of the human person?

If we answer "yes" to these questions, as we should, then we should proceed with confidence in asserting not just that the Church should influence politics, but that politics simply *is* the community living for and in Christ. If we really believe what we say we believe about the incoherence and inhumaneness of secular liberalism, then of course we shouldn't worry about accommodating Church teaching and authority to the status quo. Rather, we should be trying to fill the void left by sterile secularism in the hearts of every person.

Around the Western world, people are looking for something with substance and rigor to believe in. The cosmopolitanism of our elite only works for the elite—those with power and privilege who can access the benefits of the apex of the social hierarchy. (But even there, of course, unease and emptiness dominate.) Some have latched onto national and ethnic identities as a source of transcendent meaning. Others have found community and structure in fringe-but-growing cults, such as Scientology and Neopaganism. Still others have found in political Islam a feeling of certainty and security that eluded them in the always-skeptical but never-committal West. (A significant number of Islamic State recruits were European young men.)

So we shouldn't be trying to piggyback on the dying liberal order. If there was ever a time when accommodating secular liberalism might come with some benefits—and there probably wasn't—that time is long past. Secularism and liberalism and relativism and postmodernism and all the other inhumane -isms of our age have left an entire civilization dazed and confused. Now is the time to speak Catholic truth with clarity and boldness. It's what the people want, and more importantly, it's what they need.

And the Catholic Church has an advantage over all the other ideologies and factions jockeying to fill the current vacuum: the Church actually has the truth. But it gets better. "The truth" is more than an abstraction: the Church offers the opportunity for relationship with the Person who is "the way, and the truth, and the life" (Jn 14:6).

Remember the words of Jesus at the Sermon on the Mount:

> A city set on a hill cannot be hidden. Nor do men light a lamp and put it under a bushel, but on a stand, and it gives light to all in the house. Let your light so shine before men, that they may see your good works and give glory to your Father who is in heaven. (Mt 5:14–16)

The faith is the light we have to offer the world, and Jesus is light itself. Let us not hide Him under the bushel of shame in the radicalness of His message. He can give light to our civilization just as He did to a dying and decadent Rome. But we have to do our part to spread that light.

*   *   *

Nowhere is the distinctiveness of what Christ and His Church have to offer the world clearer than in the sacraments—the moments when the order of nature and the order of grace intersect. The deep humanity of ritual and symbolism come together with the awesome divinity of the Holy Spirit to make the sacraments the most perfect experiences we can have in this life.

Jesus Christ is what the Church has to offer our society, and in the sacraments His life breaks into our world in a way that is perfectly suited to our embodied nature. The sacraments, therefore, are the central feature of Christian life so long as our bodies occupy space and time. And so it is through the sacraments that the Church constitutes political society.

CHAPTER 14

A Sacramental Society

A truly Catholic society will be ordered toward the common good—that good that is proper to political communities, that both includes and enhances the good of each individual, and that is therefore not diminished by anyone's participation in it. But this only makes sense if we understand some basic truths about political society.

No one is born as an individual: we are all born into a family of some kind or another. But the family ties don't end at the front door. Modern political thinking errs gravely not just in separating the individual from the family, but in separating individual families from the wider family of society as a whole.

I said earlier that the family is a universal hermeneutic, but it is also a *universal metaphysic*. The concept of the family is not just an interpretive key for understanding human societies; it also *describes* human societies simply yet profoundly. Political society is, in a sense, an extended (and often dysfunctional) family. And so we should feel comfortable speaking of the common good of a society, just as we are in speaking of the common good of our own families.

In the order of nature, the common good includes elements such as solidarity (discussed in the last chapter) and justice, by which each person is given what is due to him. This does not only refer to the punishment meted out as criminal justice, but also to the basic necessities to which every person has a natural right under distributive justice. In a properly ordered society as in a properly ordered family, no one's good is diminished when an indigent is provided with food and shelter—even if that provision has to come from someone who is better off. For the community to ignore the poor would be like a family ignoring its own hungry children; if a family simply cannot feed its children or a community cannot raise up its poor, then a higher level of authority must intervene so that justice and the common good might be served. Remember that striking admonition: "Truly, I say to you, as you did it to one of the least of these *my brethren*, you did it to me" (Mt 25:40; emphasis added).

This distribution of the fruits of a community's labor is what the Church refers to as the "universal destination of goods." While private property has its place, of course, when the first duty of a society is to ensure its productivity, every person is then allowed to enjoy a basic level of food, shelter, leisure, and so forth. This is the heart of Catholic social teaching, as laid out in documents like Leo XIII's *Rerum Novarum*, Pius XI's *Quadragesimo Anno*, John Paul II's *Centisimus Annus*, and Benedict XVI's *Deus Caritas Est*. In solidarity with our fellow human beings, we should grieve poverty without hesitation and celebrate the restoration of the poor to dignified circumstances without reservation— and work to bring as many as possible to that station.

The title of Benedict XVI's encyclical mentioned above—*Deus Caritas Est*—means "God is Love." Love is what God *does* because love is what God *is*. This isn't just a nice theological observation: we, as the family of God, must reflect and radiate this love not just in our private households but throughout the political community. Therefore, we can say that love animates all our family ties: "Beloved, let us love one another; for love is of God, and he who loves is born of God and knows God" (1 Jn 4:7).

The focus of this chapter will be primarily the common good in the order of grace—the supernatural common good. The natural common good reflects the superabundance of God's love and mercy, but can never replicate or replace it. (Attempts to replace the gratuity of God's grace with the power of the state or market always end in injustice and excess.) The supernatural common good, however, is our participation in the life of Christ.

This participation culminates in salvation—eternal blissful communion with Jesus Christ. While we cannot be saved by a political or social order, any order organized without an eye fixed on heaven ignores the purpose of human existence. It's like stocking a professional basketball team only with tall men who can't shoot, or casting a movie only with beautiful models who can't act: things might look all right at first, but it soon becomes clear that you've missed the point of the endeavor. It turns out that the Church is in her very nature a social order—indeed a perfect social order. I will call this order "the sacramental society."

*   *   *

The sacramental society is the integrated society—the one in which the integrated truth of man's nature is reflected in society. We are spirit *and* body: both should be served by the political community. We are political *and* spiritual: these two aspects of our nature cannot be compartmentalized. We have duties to God *and* to our fellow men: these duties are inextricably intertwined and belong to every member of the community.

In other words, the sacramental society recognizes that Jesus Christ is Lord and that His Church is not an institution vying for earthly power, but the manifestation on earth of the reality of heaven. The reality of the sacraments cannot simply season the life of the community with a little divine intervention now and again. They are portals to the deeper supernatural reality of human existence, one which can transform us and our communities if, through a radical openness to the Holy Spirit, we permit it.

It is heartbreaking that we moderns have become accustomed to seeing the sacraments simply as interludes of "spirituality" in our lives—as breaks from "regular life." When we go to Mass or to Confession, we feel like we're stepping out of the "real world" into the world of the Church. When we attend the Baptism or Confirmation or Matrimony of a friend or family member, it feels like a special occasion, not just in the sense that these sacraments are once-in-a-lifetime celebrations but also in the sense that "religious duties" are breaking in on everyday life.

On one hand, of course, this is good and natural: the sacraments *are* special moments where God's presence is manifested in a unique and tangible way. On the other hand, however, this suggests an unnatural distinction between the life of the Church and the rest of life. The sacraments should be part of our everyday experience, not magical interludes in an otherwise secular existence.

A society organized around the sacraments makes the truths of the faith part of everyday life. For instance, the sacraments take their form from covenant oaths, by which ancient pacts were sealed. Covenants weren't simply contracts, though; these were the type of permanent agreements by which families were formed and clans expanded—marriages, adoptions, and so forth. And God was always considered to be part of the covenant. The sacraments, then, are reaffirmations of God's familial covenant with His people.[1]

Therefore, the sacraments also instantiate the Trinitarian nature of God in everyday life. There are three persons acting in every sacrament: the person ministering the sacrament, the person receiving the sacrament, and God. (In Matrimony, the couple serves as both ministers and recipients of the sacrament; thus marriage is a covenant specifically among the spouses and God.) Of course, in every sacrament we invoke the Trinitarian nature of God: Father, Son, and Holy Spirit. In Baptism, this Trinitarian formulation is *essential* to the sacrament; for this reason the Church does not recognize baptisms performed by non-Trinitarian religious groups, such as the Church of Jesus Christ of Latter Day Saints (Mormonism) and Jehovah's Witnesses.

Most importantly, the sacraments bring the truth of salvation into the daily lives of the community. The sacraments should be at the center of community life because

---

[1]   See *Swear to God*, ch. 5.

SCOTT HAHN

they are essential to eternal life. It doesn't get much simpler than that.

* * *

But let's bring the sacraments back to earth for a moment. These are the moments where heaven and earth intersect, so their impact is not merely in the spiritual realm. The natural and supernatural elements of the common good reinforce one another in a special way through the sacraments. Specifically, the sacraments are the surest source and sustainer of solidarity. Here let's focus on three sacraments that usually take place at different times in a person's life journey: Baptism, Confirmation, and Anointing of the Sick.

Baptism not only initiates a person, usually an infant, into the family of Christ in a spiritual sense; it initiates the person into the Christian community here on earth. The baptized truly becomes a brother or sister in Christ. This familial relationship reinforces and elevates the kinship of the political society. Further, it reminds us of the interconnectedness discussed by St. John Paul II in the previous chapter—and it therefore comes with special responsibilities. Remember the words of St. Peter: "Honor all men. *Love the brotherhood*" (1 Pet 2:17; emphasis added).

Confirmation is the next sacrament of initiation. While the age at which Confirmation is administered has changed through time—for most of Church history it *preceded* Communion—it has always been associated with the use of reason. That is, Confirmation is when the faithful affirm for themselves their membership in the Body of Christ. The outpouring of the Holy Spirit *completes* and *perfects* baptismal grace, leaving "an indelible spiritual mark" that raises the confirmand fully to the "common priesthood of the faithful" (CCC 1304–05). Thus, the grace of the sacrament brings with it special duties and the special capabilities with which to fulfill those duties.

Both of these sacraments of initiation affirm membership in the family of God—the special solidarity of the faithful. This is affirmed even further in the customarily public nature of these sacraments; they are performed in the presence of the community who both witness to and pledge to uphold the complete initiation of the new brother or sister in Christ. In a sacramental society, the full social meaning of this initiation would be more tangible than it is now, when parents and teenagers often see the sacrament as the *culmination* of their duty to the Church and fellow Christians rather than the *beginning*.

In the Anointing of the Sick, then, we see both the efficacious outpouring of grace on the afflicted and a solemn reminder of our duties to the aged and infirm. The elderly, in particular, are increasingly invisible to society and even to their own families in nursing homes and hospices; this sacrament makes them visible again as subjects of solidarity to whom we owe support not just in view of their age or experience or accomplishments, but in view of their humanity.

Anointing of the Sick does not *complete* the cycle of solidarity begun in Baptism, because we have further duties to the dying and the dead—especially prayers for the souls in purgatory. But it does point toward the cradle-to-grave duties we have to our Christian family. The sacraments are both effective instruments and reminders of the solidarity we owe to all persons.

*   *   *

Sacramentum, as I have said, is Latin for "oath." The concept of an oath—a solemn commitment enforced not just by the civil law but by God Himself—is totally foreign to our secular liberal society. To us, all commitments are "contracts," and all contracts are breakable with enough gumption and clever lawyers. The only duties we have are those we choose, and if our choices change, well, everyone else needs to adjust to our new preferences. This means constant social rancor, and in the end we all have to conform ourselves to the choices of the powerful—those who can assert their preferences most effectively.

Covenantal oaths—that is, the sacraments—offer a source of social cohesion unimaginable under secular liberalism. They are lifelong commitments in which God participates. This second part is essential to the first: without God, covenantal commitments are too much for fallen human beings to handle.

I've explored this already in the context of marriage, and the Sacrament of Matrimony is a prime example of this point: the marriage *covenant* gives a substance and structure to society that a breakable *contract* cannot—let alone a renewable "wed lease," as has been recently proposed. In a sacramental society, the sacramental understanding of marriage would be assumed; it would be "just the way things are," in the way rampant divorce, prenuptial agreements, and so forth are "just the way things are" now.

Let's turn, then, to another sacrament where the participation of the Lord offers us something inconceivable under our current regime: Confession. Confession is, of course, the most private sacrament. The confessional is one of the last remaining places in our culture where one can be assured of privacy and confidentiality; it is therefore one of the last remaining places where we are able to speak out loud the hardest truths—our most personal temptations, weaknesses, and failings. But it is exactly for this reason that it is so socially important.

Confession isn't just therapeutic—though the act of confessing is psychologically healthy. We get more than a peaceful feeling of relief from the sacrament; we are truly healed and forgiven by the Lord Jesus Christ. He is a participant in the sacrament, beckoning us always back into His covenantal friendship.

This kind of radical forgiveness is unthinkable in the secular world. The only forgiveness we can conceive of is the uncertain and contingent forgiveness of our fellow men, and so we despair of the possibility of ever being truly made whole again. If we can't be forgiven in the radical sense offered by divine mercy, then why try to be good at all? This inability to experience forgiveness is one of the great sources of despair in the modern world.

And it is therefore one of the great sources of social discord. Sacramental confession doesn't just heal us in isolation; the grace of the sacrament prepares us to approach all our relationships and communal duties with the confidence that can only come from God's love working through us. His mercy grants us a unique and radical peacefulness that makes social peace possible.

*   *   *

What does it mean for society that at every Mass the Body, Blood, Soul, and Divinity of Jesus Christ is manifested in the form of the Eucharist?

If we really believe this is the case, then the implications are enormous. The Eucharist shouldn't be just the centerpiece of every Sunday or of our "religious lives"; it should be the centerpiece of our public acts and social order. We should organize every other human concern around the Real Presence of our Lord in the Blessed Sacrament. This is what it means to take seriously the words of the fathers of the Second Vatican Council that the Eucharist is "the source and summit of the Christian life."[2]

It's awkward to say this because we're so accustomed to separating "religion" from "politics," but if we really believe what we say we believe about the Eucharist, then the Mass is necessarily a *political act*. The implications of God breaking into our lives in such a dramatic way cannot be contained by the hour of the Mass or the four walls of the church. The Mass brings the King of the Universe into our midst in a tangible way that no other ritual or even other sacrament could. It would be far more foolish to consider the Mass nonpolitical than to admit the obvious: liturgy and politics cannot be disentangled.

Mass is the central community event in the sacramental society. Corporate worship—that is, worship of the Trinitarian God as the Body of Christ—is the most important action a community can undertake. Worship orients the community vertically, toward heaven, and the Eucharist

---

[2] Second Vatican Council, Dogmatic Constitution on the Church *Lumen Gentium* (November 21, 1964), §11.

bestows the grace needed to sustain that orientation. "Horizontal" concerns—that is, aspects of life that are primarily about humans interacting with one another in the worldly plane, such as economics and athletics and social lives—should give way to the preeminence of the vertical. In so doing, those "worldly" concerns can be elevated and transfigured by grace.

*   *   *

Imagine a world where the Sacrament of Holy Orders is commonplace. Imagine attending ordinations with nearly the same frequency with which you attend baptisms and confirmations and weddings. Imagine seeing the priesthood not as a strange aberration but as a live option for every young man growing in the faith.

The sacramental society is a priestly society, and the priestly society is a servant society. The Catechism tells us that "The ordained ministry or *ministerial* priesthood is at the service of the baptismal priesthood [Cf. LG 10 §2]" (1120). Holy Orders is one of two sacraments "directed toward the salvation of others; if they contribute as well to personal salvation, it is through service to others that they do so" (CCC 1534). What is the other sacrament that has this quality? It is Matrimony, in which the spouses' primary duty is in service to one another; in the same way they confer the sacrament on each other, they also sanctify each other. It is for this reason, also, that we can say that marriage and the priesthood are radically *political* vocations.

The apostolic nature of the ministerial priesthood brings Christ into our world, both in the form of the Eucharist and in the form of the other duties, such as the Sacrament of Confession, in which the priest acts *in persona Christi*. The sacramental society is thus also an apostolic society, reaching backwards in time to Christ's first coming and forward in time to His second coming. He is never out of view, and He is not an abstraction but a *person* whose presence is real and powerful.

A robust culture of priesthood also reminds us that the traditional and proper division between the religious and secular realms of society is not church and state, but clergy and laity. Rather than being set in opposition to one another, as in the church–state understanding, these two orders are to support one another in prayer and service. The laity and the clergy—the baptismal priesthood and the ministerial priesthood—are not competing poles of authority but complementary orders in the service of the only final authority: Jesus Christ and His Church.

*   *   *

This is the sacramental society: the social order not just implied by but *contained in* the universal Church, continually imbued with sacramental grace. It is the society most in accord with the reality of the Church. It is the society that takes seriously what Catholics believe about God, mankind, and the covenantal relationship between us.

You see, there is no social order that is not also an ecclesial order. Whether we acknowledge it or not, the Church is all around us at all times—not institutionally or bureaucratically, but in the order of grace. Even the most egregiously secular culture still interacts with the saints and the angels;

the relationship is simply one of conflict rather than cooperation. The question is not "Shall we incorporate the Church into our social order?" but "*How* shall we incorporate the Church into our social order?"

We don't speak abstractly or metaphorically when we say that Christ is alive and that He suffuses our world with His grace through His bride, the Church. That's the way the world is, whether we see it or not. That so many people—even many Catholics—do not know that the Church is in fact all around us is one of the greatest tragedies of modernity. But to accept that truth is one of the greatest graces imaginable, and it is one that can heal, perfect, and elevate our floundering civilization.

So we can expand on the insight of the great philosophers and theologians that man is a social animal by saying that man is an *ecclesial animal*. We cannot escape having a relationship with Christ and His Church; it is simply part of being human. We have to choose whether we will work *with* the relationship of love Christ desires to have with us, or *against* it. The latter leads not just to personal ruin but to societal discord. The former leads to salvation and is the kernel of the sacramental society. Christ is the only sure foundation for social peace and civilizational flourishing.

The sacramental society is ordered to both the temporal and spiritual common good of mankind. It gives us all that we need to live fully human lives both here on earth and after death. Thus it is *good in itself* that we try to build it. And if it really is as good as we say it is, others will be drawn to it.

This is not easy or mainstream or respectable. It will come with costs, social, economic, and personal. But so do all good things in bad times. And God will, as He always has, reward the effort on His behalf.

CHAPTER 15

Conclusion: Beyond Reach?

If at times the argument of this book has felt speculative, even a bit fanciful, that is understandable. The social and ecclesial vision laid out in these pages, though grounded in the accessible and concrete truth of marriage, is by contemporary standards utterly radical, and history provides us with no "proofs of concept" (with the arguable exception of certain medieval societies).[1] There is no roadmap, in this book or anywhere else, that will lead us directly and assuredly to the sacramental society.

But this should not cause us to despair any more than the other utterly radical demands of the Catholic faith lead us to despair. As we described in detail earlier in this book, Christian marriage isn't just radical but *impossible* without

---

[1] See Andrew Willard Jones, *Before Church and State: A Study of Social Order in the Sacramental Kingdom of St. Louis IX* (Steubenville, OH: Emmaus Academic, 2017) for a historical sketch of thirteenth century France under King St. Louis IX, which may have been the closest we have come to organizing a truly sacramental society.

the purifying and strengthening grace of the Lord. Indeed, Jesus Christ calls us to a perfection that our human nature cannot achieve on its own, but which *can be* given to us by the God who is Love.

Bringing the sacramental civilization into being, therefore, is not so much a question of *building* as it is a question of *accepting* what is being offered to us by Christ from above. Through grace and the mediation of the saints and angels, who make up the perfect society of heaven, we can participate in His life right here and now.

The first step is not political or electoral but, appropriately, familial and marital. By allowing that first society to be elevated and transformed by grace, we set the conditions for a reverberation of grace across our communities and across the generations. Rather than fussing about when "society" is going to get its act together, the Church—including and especially the laity living out the Sacrament of Marriage— needs to get its act together. We need to accept the lordship of Jesus Christ through radical openness to the Holy Spirit before we can expect our society to be transformed by His power and love.

That means dioceses and parishes ordering their work first and foremost to the sacramental life of the Church, but it also means *living sacramentally* ourselves—not just partaking of the sacraments regularly, which is of course essential, but organizing our lives around the covenantal love of Jesus made available to us in a unique way through the Church. Then *we* become the proofs of concept for those around us looking to participate in a more just and beautiful social order. Recall the beautiful words of Pope Benedict XVI in the epigraph to this book:

Matrimony is a Gospel in itself, a Good News for the world of today, especially the dechristianized world. The union of a man and a woman, their becoming "one flesh" in charity, in fruitful and indissoluble love, is a sign that speaks of God with a force and an eloquence which in our days has become greater. . . . And it is not by chance. Marriage is linked to faith, but not in a general way. Marriage, as a union of faithful and indissoluble love, is based upon the grace that comes from the triune God, who in Christ loved us with a faithful love, even to the Cross.

If you feel challenged and convicted in reading these words, know that I do as well. The kind of radical obedience required to live this vision of marriage and of society isn't just in deep conflict with contemporary culture; it's in deep conflict with our fallen nature. But grace heals, perfects, and elevates that nature; grace brings the apparently impossible within our reach.

And so our personal, marital, and familial witness is *the* essential element in the sacramental society. No institution or set of rules and regulations can bring it about; it requires holy, virtuous people who form holy, virtuous families that in turn form holy, virtuous societies. Individuals striving to become saints is the only way to have a society worthy of the saints.

*   *   *

In the thirty-ninth chapter of the Book of Isaiah, the great prophet tells Hezekiah, king of Israel, that someday the Babylonians will plunder the wealth of his kingdom and enslave his people. But the king, who knows from God that he will only live fifteen more years, coolly responds, "'The word of the LORD which you have spoken is good.' For he thought, 'There will be peace and security in my days'" (Is 39:8).

The only time horizon Hezekiah cared about was his own death; nothing mattered after that. We can't fall into this kind of thinking. Remember that part of the universality of the Church is its continuity *through time*. The family of God goes down through the ages; therefore we have duties looking backward and, even more importantly, looking forward beyond our own lives.

While this is certainly a great responsibility, it should also be a great comfort. Surely nothing like the social vision laid out in this book will come to pass in our lifetime (barring a miraculous intervention by the Lord Himself). But rather than despair over this, let's sow some seeds—or at least prepare the soil. Let's start to lay a foundation—or at least clear the rubble.

In other words: let's avoid surrendering essential first principles and compromising the faith for short-term reprieves. We're probably not going to witness any spectacular mass conversion to sanctity in our lifetimes, so let's be heroic in accepting short-term humiliation—only an *apparent* defeat—without compromise. This would be, in fact, no small victory; it might even be precisely the foundation of witnesses to holiness on which future generations build something more beautiful than we can now imagine.

*　*　*

I have been happy to concede that the vision of this book is, by any customary standard, unrealistic and extravagant. But so is eternal communion with the all-powerful and all-knowing Lord of Hosts, and yet we know by faith that this is not only *possible*—it's what we were made for. But it is only possible by grace.

This is, therefore, not a utopian vision, at least not in the traditional sense of that word. We cannot achieve an enduring society committed to justice and the common good by our own efforts. The allure of sin and the murkiness of unaided human reason will always lead us to make unacceptable compromises of life and liberty—usually at the expense of the weakest—in the name of some "greater good" that bears no resemblance to the common good. This is what is happening all around us, as we sacrifice the rights of those least able to protect themselves in the name of prosperity, security, autonomy, ethnic purity, or whatever the current idol of the elite might be.

But isn't this also the story of every human life, every marriage, and every family? Aren't we always tempted to embrace sin for the sake of some "greater good," some idol that has supplanted God in our lives? Don't we always fail, no matter how hard we seem to try? And yet this does not give us a license to stop reaching, working, striving for perfection!

St. Paul's Second Letter to the Corinthians is shot through with admonitions not to despair, since our strength comes from the Lord. In the third chapter he writes that "we are [not] sufficient of ourselves to claim anything as coming from us; our sufficiency is from God, who has qualified us to be ministers of a new covenant" (2 Cor 3:5–6). In the next chapter, he fixes his gaze and ours on Christ: "We are afflicted in every way, but not crushed; perplexed, but not driven to despair; persecuted, but not forsaken; struck down, but not destroyed; always carrying in the body the death of Jesus, so that the life of Jesus may also be manifested in our bodies" (2 Cor 4:8–10). And later on he reveals to us those beautiful words spoken to him by the Lord Himself: "My grace is sufficient for you, for my power is made perfect in weakness" (2 Cor 12:9).

The sacramental society is impossible in the same way the first society of marriage is impossible and in the same way sainthood is impossible: all of these are ruled out by our fallen nature and, miraculously, brought within reach through surrender to the will and grace of God. Indeed, the Letter to the Hebrews describes Jesus Christ not just as perfect but as the "perfecter":

> Therefore, since we are surrounded by so great a cloud of witnesses, let us also lay aside every weight, and sin which clings so closely, and let us run with perseverance the race that is set before us, looking to Jesus the pioneer and perfecter of our faith, who for the joy that was set before him endured the cross, despising the shame, and is seated at the right hand of the throne of God. (Heb 12:1–2)

* * *

Let us turn now to that "cloud of witnesses." No account of the Church and of human society is complete without discussing the Church Triumphant—the saints in heaven who support us with their prayers and inspire us, the Church Militant, with their example.

Here we find the proof of concept that eludes us in earthly history: the saints and holy angels transfigured by His grace and transfixed by His beauty are living the reality that we aim for right now. And the wonderful truth is that we *can* share in that reality here on earth. In fact, we do so every time we participate in Holy Mass—the Marriage Supper of the Lamb promised to us in heaven of which we are granted a foretaste.

And so while this vision of a society saturated by the love and grace of Christ might not be practically achievable in customary terms, *it is inevitable*. It is the deeper truth of all human civilization, indeed of all human existence. The heavenly realm has always been and will always be. Everything we experience here on earth is merely a dim reflection of that reality, that perfection, that existence. And, God willing, we will someday encounter the genuine article—the unobscured divinity of the Holy Trinity. As St. Paul says, "For now we see in a mirror dimly, but then face to face" (1 Cor 13:12).

*   *   *

It is most profitable, then, to think of this vision of marriage and society not as a faraway goal to achieve, but rather as an accounting of what we already have available to us—both in the sacraments of the Church here on earth and in the community of saints in heaven. In this way, this sketch I have proposed is both *Catholic* and *catholic*, that is, universal. It embraces reality in its fullness, both seen and unseen by mortal eyes. It refuses to be hemmed in by modern ideologies that ignore or deny the relevance or even the existence of the heavenly state of divine communion.

Marriage, you see, is not just the first society, but also, in its transfigured and divinized form, the last society. It is both the form and the fundamental unit of all human societies—the universal metaphysic—precisely because it is the earthly analogue for divine communion. It is the universal interpretive key for understanding our experience and our nature because it is the interpretive key for understanding our relationship with our Creator. It is the most fundamentally and undeniably human relationship because it is a reflection of and participation in the divine relationship among the persons of the Trinity and the citizens of heaven—a perfect and eternal communion of persons.

How can we possibly respond with anything but awe at the magnificence of this truth and gratitude for the grace of God and the sacraments of the Church, which make this participation in the divine life possible? And then how, once we have embraced this awe and gratitude, can we do anything other than commit to ordering our lives on the terms of heaven—that is, around the grace-filled and covenantal reality of the sacraments?

When we do this—and *only* when we do this—can we begin to invoke, discern, and draw power from the heavenly reality for our work here on earth. Only then can the first society of humanity begin to approach the splendor of the last society of heaven. And only then can we begin to see a more just, more fulfilling, more perfect civilization emerge from the devastation of a culture scoured by secularism.